Changing Academic Work

SRHE and Open University Press Imprint
General Editor: Heather Eggins

Current titles include:

Catherine Bargh, Peter Scott and David Smith: *Governing Universities*
Ronald Barnett: *Improving Higher Education: Total Quality Care*
Ronald Barnett: *The Idea of Higher Education*
Ronald Barnett: *The Limits of Competence*
Ronald Barnett: *Higher Education: A Critical Business*
John Biggs: *Teaching for Quality Learning at University*
John Bird: *Black Students and Higher Education*
Jean Bocock and David Watson (eds): *Managing the Curriculum*
David Boud *et al.* (eds): *Using Experience for Learning*
Etienne Bourgeois *et al.*: *The Adult University*
John Brennan *et al.* (eds): *What Kind of University?*
Angela Brew (ed.): *Directions in Staff Development*
Anne Brockbank and Ian McGill: *Facilitating Reflective Learning in Higher Education*
Ann Brooks: *Academic Women*
Sally Brown and Angela Glasner (eds): *Assessment Matters in Higher Education*
Robert G. Burgess (ed.): *Beyond the First Degree*
Frank Coffield and Bill Williamson (eds): *Repositioning Higher Education*
John Cowan: *On Becoming an Innovative University Teacher*
Rob Cuthbert (ed.): *Working in Higher Education*
Heather Eggins (ed.): *Women as Leaders and Managers in Higher Education*
Gillian Evans: *Calling Academia to Account*
David Farnham (ed.): *Managing Academic Staff in Changing University Systems*
Sinclair Goodlad: *The Quest for Quality*
Harry Gray (ed.): *Universities and the Creation of Wealth*
Diana Green (ed.): *What is Quality in Higher Education?*
Elaine Martin: *Changing Academic Work*
Robin Middlehurst: *Leading Academics*
Sarah Neal: *The Making of Equal Opportunities Policies in Universities*
David Palfreyman and David Warner (eds): *Higher Education and the Law*
Moira Peelo: *Helping Students with Study Problems*
John Pratt: *The Polytechnic Experiment*
Michael Prosser and Keith Trigwell: *Understanding Learning and Teaching*
Yoni Ryan and Ortrun Zuber-Skerritt: *Supervising Postgraduates from Non-English Speaking Backgrounds*
Tom Schuller (ed.): *The Changing University?*
Peter Scott: *The Meanings of Mass Higher Education*
Peter Scott (ed.): *The Globalization of Higher Education*
Harold Silver and Pamela Silver: *Students*
Anthony Smith and Frank Webster (eds): *The Postmodern University?*
Imogen Taylor: *Developing Learning in Professional Education*
Susan Toohey: *Designing Courses for Higher Education*
Paul R. Trowler: *Academics Responding to Change*
David Warner and Elaine Crosthwaite (eds): *Human Resource Management in Higher and Further Education*
David Warner and Charles Leonard: *The Income Generation Handbook* (Second Edition)
David Warner and David Palfreyman (eds): *Higher Education Management*
Graham Webb: *Understanding Staff Development*
Sue Wheeler and Jan Birtle: *A Handbook for Personal Tutors*

Changing Academic Work

Developing the Learning University

Elaine Martin

The Society for Research into Higher Education
& Open University Press

Published by SRHE and
Open University Press
Celtic Court
22 Ballmoor
Buckingham
MK18 1XW

email: enquiries@openup.co.uk
world wide web: http://www.openup.co.uk

and 325 Chestnut Street
Philadelphia, PA19106, USA

First published 1999

A catalogue record of this book is available from the British Library

ISBN 0 335 19883 X (pbk)   0 335 19884 8 (hbk)

Library of Congress Cataloging-in-Publication Data

Martin, Elaine. 1948–
Changing academic work: developing the learning university/Elaine Martin.
p. cm.
Includes bibliographical references (p.) and index.
ISBN 0-335-19884-8 (hb)
ISBN 0-335-19883-X (pb)
1. Education, Higher. 2. College teaching. 3. College teachers—Job stress. 4. Educational change. I. Title.
LA184 .M37 1999
B78—ddc21   98-45149
CIP

Typeset by Graphicraft Limited, Hong Kong
Printed in Great Britain by St Edmundsbury Press,
Bury St Edmunds, Suffolk

Contents

Preface

A vice-chancellor of my acquaintance presided over the closing of five departments in his university and then joked that if he heard one more story about low morale he would cry. To me, it seemed a very black joke, the anxiety and distress of the staff in this university was no laughing matter.

Around the same time, I attended a seminar where a colleague made a plea for academic staff to stand firm and resist all further changes in academic work. This seemed an equally misguided statement. A life with no change, no development, would surely be a very limited life.

In stressful times it is common for people to adopt extreme positions and become defensive rather than cooperative and these are stressful times. To observe academic staff behave in these ways, however, is disturbing. University people, at all levels, are very often exceptional men and women of great personal capacity. Working together they can be an awesome force; working against each other they are destructive.

I believed that a book to help academic staff to work together in these difficult times would be a worthwhile endeavour.

I am, above all else, a teacher and, as I saw it, staff in universities had a lot of learning to do: a lot of learning about the global and changing demands on higher education; a lot of learning about what these changes mean for working differently; and a lot of learning about helping themselves and colleagues to let go of traditional and valued practices and begin working together in a new and different tertiary climate.

As an exponent and contributor to the student learning literature, I believed that much of the student learning literature was relevant. Later, as I read more, I saw that the literature on learning organizations and on organizational change was equally relevant. The way forward, in theory at least, appeared to be to apply these two literatures to key issues of change in universities. I had my own idea about what the key issues were but I believed the best place to start was with the experiences of staff themselves and I undertook a survey of staff in the UK and in Australia. When I did this I found, as one always finds, that things were not exactly as expected. The key issues were not that different to those anticipated but the intensity of feeling generated by staff was unexpected and, at times, alarming.

Around this time I attended a three-day workshop run by the late Donald Schön. In this workshop we explored his work, and that of his friend and colleague, Chris Argyris, on working through difficult situations. This work was influential in helping me find the distinctive voice of the book.

Perhaps the most significant factor in finding this voice has been my own illness. I wrote the book whilst undergoing a series of treatments for cancer and during this time I came to know three things profoundly. The first was the value and brevity of life. The second was the need to have purpose in our relatively short lives. The third was that, in the last analysis, we are on our own. Circumstances and friends and colleagues may often be supportive, but we cannot expect this – and, in the end, we rely on ourselves. The book, consequently, became charged with a notion of finding purpose and value in our work; of balancing self-help and autonomy with collaboration with colleagues; of valuing the past but preparing for a future.

Elaine Martin
Melbourne

Acknowledgements

First of all, I owe a lot to the academic staff who responded to my survey. Without their input there could not have been a book. Their comments emphasized just how busy they were, and yet they generously found the time to respond openly and fully. Second, I am indebted to those staff who spent time working with me on the case studies. As well as those staff whose experiences (though not real names) are included there are others whose stories have not been drawn upon. I am indebted to all of these staff, for their time, patience and trust.

I owe a further debt to those other academic staff who have been my students (in a graduate certificate/diploma course on university teaching and learning) and whose interviews with their own students I have drawn upon.

I began writing this book with Joan Benjamin as co-author and the book's conception owes much to her. It has been a great regret that my own ill health and her busy schedule meant that the book could not be pursued collaboratively.

I have written this book over a period of two-and-a-half years and for much of that time I have been undergoing treatment for cancer. In many ways the experience of treatment and that of writing the book have become one and those who supported and assisted me in writing the book invariably supported me during difficult times of the illness. My immediate colleagues at work require a special mention here: John Bowden, Carmen Heliotis, John Milton, Kate Patrick and Peter Ling; not only did they take on my work load – but graciously allowed me to have some input – as I was able.

My special friend and colleague Helen Lennox supported me in many thoughtful ways both at home and at work. My colleague and friend Michael Prosser gave me support and confidence by talking through and helping me to clarify ideas.

It has not been an easy time for my son and daughter, Leo and Helen. I thank them for their patience with my moods and depression. I also thank Leo for his professional help with literature searching and referencing.

I owe a special debt to Paul Ramsden and Cassandra O'Brien who have both read several drafts of the book. Paul has brought to the book an exacting intellectual criticism, which has significantly improved the final product. Cassandra has painstakingly worked to help identify inconsistencies and get the book into final draft form. She has been the most steadfast of colleagues and friends. Her support has been invaluable.

1

Changes in Academic Work

Every new truth which has ever been propounded has, for a time, caused mischief . . . and if the truth is very great as well as very new, the harm is serious.

(Henry Buckle)

Introduction

All of us involved in university life know that higher education has had to change in recent times and while we might acknowledge that some of that change has been necessary, and even praiseworthy, most of us would recognize that change has come at a price. Universities may now be more efficient; they may serve a more diverse range of students and be more closely linked to the needs of business and industry – but there are significant proportions of academic staff who are disillusioned, who feel ill-equipped to deal with contemporary demands and who feel at odds with the new values and practices of their particular university. It is not easy for academic staff to think positively about the future when there is little time to do the things which seem worthwhile, when long-cherished values concerning professional practice and academic freedom are challenged and when one's colleagues are profoundly dispirited and stressed.

Changes in work in the larger community

Changes in academic work have, of course, to be seen in the context of changes in work practices within the community at large. It is easy to forget the bigger picture when we are engrossed in our own problems. There may be no increase in staff to give tutorials to the first years, only an increase in demands for documentation concerning curriculum and learning outcomes – but, equally, there are no longer conductors to take our fares and to help the infirm on and off public transport; no-one to offer palliative care in hospitals or nursing homes – and these areas, too, feel the pressure for increased accountability despite a decline in staffing.

Business now, both in the public and private sector, has become serious, efficient and economically sound. Jobs which make economic sense are the ones which are maintained. Work which is not central and essential one hundred per cent of the time is exported. Instead of maintaining a workforce group set aside for training, for caring or supporting and for handling emergencies, this workforce is situated outside of the organization as consultants, as temporary workers and is called in on a contract basis when needed (Handy 1996). If we return to our own situation in the universities, around half of our academic staff are currently employed on such a basis – and the trend is fast growing (Coaldrake 1998).

Paradox at work

At one level, we know that the changes which are taking place are due to larger trends which originate way beyond our immediate department, unit or university – and yet, when we consider this bigger picture, it is still hard to comprehend what is happening. On the one hand, our services as teachers and researchers are apparently less crucial; they can be pulled in or pushed out of institutions according to the ebb and flow of specific programmes; but, on the other hand, we know that we are now part of a mass higher education system with more students undertaking higher levels of education and needing more support to learn. Our services appear to be both more in demand and, yet, less essential.

We also realize that we are now in the information age – the next age to follow the industrial age – when the ability to both acquire and apply knowledge is the new source of status and wealth. Once, it might have been thought that academic staff would have had a full-time and significant part to play in these changes and that our services would not have been considered peripheral. We recognize that electronic technology now 'delivers' much of the information we once disseminated through lectures and printed notes, but those of us who are committed teachers know that such information – no matter how detailed – is not the same as learning. It is the 'receiving' by students – not the 'delivering' – that is crucial. Good teaching ensures students 'receive' – that they are tuned into, and make personal sense of, the information which abounds.

There is another paradox concerning work and time which emerges when we consider the consequences of this information age. Universities, like all other organizations, are now reshaping the concept of time. There are actually 168 hours in a week, not 40, so why ignore the other 128 hours? We can now visit the supermarket and shop at midnight; we can catch up on an e-mail tutorial with students at 6.00 a.m. on a Sunday morning just as we can work on the literature search via the Internet on a Saturday night. Our students are similarly liberated and have the advantage of this flexibility for study. Sometimes it seems, however, that while our life is infinitely more flexible, it is no longer *our* life. There is no time in the day or week when we are able to legitimately claim that this is *our* time for *our* life. Every moment can be filled with a commitment and we quickly find that it is and, strangely, although we now have 168 hours instead of 40, there is still not enough time.

Perhaps an even bigger paradox has been that during the 1980s the corporate aim was to walk the management path of increased control and efficiency and move towards more predictability – and by the end of the decade those firms which were best at this were those which had failed most dramatically (Peters 1988). Increased control and planning seems not to have served us too well – and yet, as university staff, as staff in any organization – it seems that more, rather than less, planning is undertaken to prepare for the future. I am still required by my university to have prepared my personal workplan; my unit still has to submit its strategic plan and all of these plans have to fit in with the university's overall plans.

Working with paradox

We are told that paradoxes abound because we are now in an age of constant change and that change and actions and reactions reverberate at such speed that stability and predictability are, at best, fragile (Senge 1992; Fullan 1994; Handy 1996). Things no longer line up in a neat and predictable way and this is not easy because our lives and our work become a package of contradictions and uncertainties. Questions concerning how we, as academic staff, contribute to society at large; how our students should benefit and what this might mean for how we work and what we work on are no longer readily answered because the larger picture is changing so quickly. It is easy to become increasingly perplexed and anxious and wary of acting at all when the fast changing circumstances mean that to act quickly is vital. This situation can be labelled 'paradox in the postmodern world' but this does not help much. We have to know how to work in this postmodern world. It especially has to be done by academic staff because we are the ones who are preparing young people for life and work in the future. We are, therefore, ill-suited for such responsibility if we are not at least minimally adept at coping with the present.

Framing the concerns of academic staff

It is a paradox in itself, that the best way to cope with the turbulence and uncertainty of contemporary life and work is to find a way to frame it in our minds (Handy 1996: 48). Often when we frame the paradoxes, we see that what we are dealing with is not so much incompatible positions or truths, but rather positions which must be constantly worked with and balanced.

We all know that good teaching, perhaps like good contemporary academic work, involves balancing freedom with guidance (or accountability) and yet, on the face of it, freedom and accountability or guidance appear to be opposites. We all know that good research involves attention to the big picture as well as to the detail. It is not a matter of either one or the other; it is a matter of both in balanced measure. Framing the apparent paradoxes, the confusion and the concerns which are most expressed by academic staff, and then helping them to balance these paradoxes or tensions is the aim of this book.

In Chapter 2, the major changes in academic work in recent years are highlighted and a report is given on how staff in universities have experienced these changes. Data from an international survey of academic staff which was conducted during 1995 and 1996 are used. The survey itself was not a large one. It involved 161 staff, at all levels of the academic profession, in the UK and Australia, but what the staff actually said is very similar to what staff have said in similar surveys; in particular, the surveys undertaken by Halsey (1992) in the UK; McInnis (1996) in Australia; and the Carnegie Foundation's extensive international survey of academic staff from 14 countries reported by Altbach (1997). The survey shows that academic staff feel undervalued, particularly as teachers. They feel that there is a lack of vision and direction concerning the overall directions of where their particular universities or institutions are going. They are particularly concerned about the lack of collaboration and a decline in traditional collegial ways of working. They are angry about the time taken up with accountability devices and argue that this accountability often appears to overshadow the main business of teaching and research. Perhaps above all, however, they are resentful at the constant demands to give more; the lack of acknowledgment of the good things which they have accomplished; and the lack of commitment to them as people. One memorable quote from a young lecturer still runs through my mind:

> I gave to my work what I should have given to my family. I now have no family . . . and I soon may have no job.

Chapter 2 ends with a summary of the main concerns of academic staff and of those in leadership positions, for while there is often concern about the same issues, these two groups offer different perspectives on the same issues. The argument develops with the claim that what university staff, leaders and non-leaders, are being asked to do is to learn new ways of working. Day-to-day academic work as it was once practised no longer fits into the demands and challenges of the contemporary university. Academic staff are not unfamiliar with learning – it is, after all, our main business – and yet, we who are university teachers and researchers often find it hard to relearn ourselves.

The literature on student learning has much which is salient to offer us here and is the focus of Chapter 3. This literature helps us to see that some learning is heuristic while some other is not, and that some of our learning environments are more likely to support the heuristic learning than are others. The challenge is to stay open to new learning.

The literature on learning organizations is the focus of Chapter 4. This learning organization literature emphasizes how stable organizations cannot survive in an unstable environment; universities which remain what they where – that is, stable as opposed to flexible – are exceedingly vulnerable. Very often, however, the organization obstructs, rather than supports, the learning of its people. People of the contemporary organization have to be supported to change and to see constant change as an essential part of their professional responsibility. But, equally, contemporary staff must learn to take responsibility themselves for their own learning and development.

In Chapter 5, the concerns of staff, together with relevant insights from the two literatures of Chapters 3 and 4, are mapped and a set of four tensions or paradoxes which academic staff have to work to balance are presented. These tensions are:

- balancing the vision or direction set by academic leaders with the day-to-day teaching and working experiences of academic staff in non-leadership positions;
- balancing the individualism which many staff pride with the need to work collaboratively;
- balancing the often heavy demands for accountability by the university with rewards within the university;
- valuing past achievements as well as preparing for a new future.

Chapters 6, 7, 8 and 9 deal with each of the above tensions, using case studies and illustrations to explore how staff have worked with these paradoxes and to summarize salient advice.

Chapter 10 is the final chapter and here the message which is constant throughout the book is made forcefully. The message is that while our experiences as academic staff have undoubtedly been painful, and while no doubt a good deal has happened which we might reasonably be angry with and demoralised by, if we want better working lives, then we must help ourselves. We cannot wait for great leaders to come and give us direction and support. The great, as always, are in short supply. Each of us must look to ourselves and expect that our own contribution, combined with that of others, will be enough to make a difference. To quote Ghandi: 'We must be the change we wish to see in the world.'

2

Experiences of Change in Academic Work

> Faced with the choice between changing one's mind and proving that there is no need to do so almost everybody gets busy on the proof.
>
> (John Kenneth Galbraith)

Introduction

A.H. Halsey (1992) in his scholarly and illuminating book, *The Decline of Donnish Dominion*, tells the complex story of the loss of status and the loss of optimism of the academic profession. The survey of 160 academic staff in the UK and Australia, undertaken in 1995 and 1996 for the present book, examines the perceptions of academic staff of their changing work and tells their own story of this demise. One respondent, familiar with Halsey's book, commented that Halsey has described the senior common room as a place, 'more interesting than joyful' (ibid.: 1). He suggested that in his own university, a former polytechnic, the senior common room was now, 'more non-existent than interesting'. The respondent, a senior physics lecturer, continued:

> The common room is now a media centre intended to be the salvation of our teaching. But, despite this salvation, we have less time than ever to do our own research or to visit a common room – and less inclination than ever to do so. There is the perception that there is no time for common room discussion and chatter, but really the issue is that there's no enthusiasm. No enthusiasm to meet with colleagues because work is no longer a joy to share. It's a burden to be borne, an unrewarding chore.

This survey of academic staff and its results are examined after some scene-setting has been done. There is no attempt here to provide an in-depth overview of the changes in higher education over the past decade; this has already been done admirably by others (see, for instance, Halsey 1992;

Marginson 1993; Scott 1995; Coaldrake 1998; Ramsden 1998). The intention is, rather, to provide a backdrop against which the comments of academic staff can be considered. This contextual backdrop is divided into a series of headings which are themselves suggested by the comments of the surveyed staff. Some of the comments from staff are also included under each heading.

The changing academic life

Reflections from the 1950s and 1960s

The life of an academic thirty or so years ago was undoubtedly a pleasant one. Classes were usually small; we are told by Halsey (1992: 99) that, on average, staff taught classes of between five and twenty students. The students in these classes were well prepared for a university education and, on the whole, were seen to be committed young men and women keen to learn and advance social progress (ibid.: 9). The teaching commitments of staff were for less than half of the weeks of the year and rarely exceeded eight hours per week.

These university teachers would have rarely published more than one article every two or three years (Halsey 1992: appendix 1, part 10b). They had no necessity to make themselves accountable or to justify what they taught or how. The profession was prestigious and confident. Neither society nor government seriously questioned their standards and values (Scott 1995: 71–2). Once appointed to an academic position, an academic staff member was there for life.

Two respondents to the survey of academic staff, undertaken for this book, recall how in the 1950s and 1960s, the academic profession remained a privileged one:

> You were seen to be special. I remember taking a train to Oxford for a conference and the guard who helped me on to the train with my bags and my books enquired of my business. When learning that I taught at a university, he escorted me to the first-class compartment and established me there. That was the proper place for university people he insisted.
>
> (Professor, history)

> Maybe we always remember our young life with nostalgia. But what I remember more than anything else were the issues and debates we had. I'm talking now about the sixties, not some distant historic time. It seemed as though being an academic was really about pursuing truth. We were passionate about it. We got results. We were not troubled with administrivia and we were not overloaded with teaching and we were not lazy, we used our time to good advantage, to do what we are best at doing, thinking and reasoning and progressing thought. I always

> savoured ideas and I was in my element as a young man who was actually paid and respected to do just that.
>
> (Professor, physics)

More universities and more students

The statistics alone tell the story. In 1961–2 in the UK there were 28 universities and 114 000 students (Halsey 1992: 95). Now the British university teacher works in system of well over a hundred universities and 1.6 million students. In Australia, in 1961, there were 57 000 students and 10 universities. Now there are 36 universities and around 640 000 students (figures based on Halsey 1992: 94; and *The National Report on Australia's Higher Education Sector* 1993). These numbers translate into classes of 100 to 200 and a staff : student ratio in some universities of 1 : 30 – once a figure unthinkable in many secondary school classrooms. But increased numbers of students in classes and the lack of opportunity for small group teaching and more individual attention is by no means the extent of the issue. A respondent to the staff survey commented on the situation in this way:

> I now teach a first-year class of 300. Around fifteen years ago, I used to teach similar subject content to a class of 30 – and was concerned, even then, that the students found the concepts difficult. I'm better at teaching it now – but not that much better. I do the best I can with these huge increases in numbers and ability levels, but I know that is not good enough and that worries me. It's bad for me and my self-esteem when my students don't learn. It's bad for the students and it's bad for the university.
>
> (Senior lecturer, chemistry)

Different students

More students means a greater variety in background and previous educational experience. Many new students will not have the same ease with abstract and theoretical ideas as did their predecessors (Coaldrake 1998). On the other hand, they may well have a facility with technological and communication packages which outstrips that of many academic staff themselves. The following comments of two survey respondents make the point:

> This year I have some students in my class and they do not write English well. They are not overseas students, they are just the sorts of students who now come to our universities. They would once have been happy to make it through secondary school, now they're in our first year. There are few books at home and they cannot make sense of an academic text. I now use videos instead of texts because they are more visually aware than they are literate. These students are not cut

> out for university education – at least not what I think of as a university education [that is] one that encourages critical analysis of complex theoretical arguments and the construction of alternative arguments but there they are and so we have to teach them.
>
> (Lecturer, social science)

> I increasingly feel at sea. I no longer am at all clear what to expect from first years. I know that I will be shocked by their inability in traditional communication. Their ability to spell, to construct grammatically correct sentences, to attend to a text, all this is so hugely wanting and I despair and yet that they are able to surf the net, to access information and to inform me is equally amazing. I am as at sea with them as no doubt they are with me.
>
> (Lecturer, English literature)

Different courses with different purposes

As well as a greater range of student background and ability, there is also a different curriculum for the expansion of the university system has not been to teach traditional knowledge from the established disciplines. The newly-developing higher education system has expanded to prepare a new workforce which can assist in the economic growth of the nation. As a survey respondent observed:

> I am in a dilemma as to what to teach, particularly at first-year level. There are so many things to balance, the ever-present demands for relevance, the concern that if you get too demanding you'll lose them. It used to be they learned chemistry and biology and the traditional disciplines in the first year, and this was seen as the basis on which practice would be developed, but now it has to be obviously relevant from the beginning, and I'm not at all sure how we can do this, and maintain the grounding they have in basic science.
>
> (Associate professor, medical laboratory science)

The newly-expanded generation of university student does not, on the whole, come to university to question and to develop theoretical ideas. They, increasingly, seek an education where the emphasis is on future employment. In Australia, enrolments in business degree courses increased 130 per cent between 1979 and 1990 (Marginson 1993). Even within traditionally non-vocational areas, such as social science, there has been a push towards vocationalism. Vocational degree courses in such areas as 'leisure and tourism', 'social work' and 'youth work' now outnumber non-vocational social science degree courses (Ashendon and Milligan 1995). A similar, though less dramatic, trend towards vocationalism can be seen in the British system (see Scott 1995: chapter 5). The comment of the following senior academic illustrates the point:

> In our interviews for selection we look out for those who are committed to getting a qualification for work rather than those who just want to study. We have to have motivated students who will work hard. We cannot afford high failure rates. We cannot afford students who might play with ideas instead of attending to the curriculum which might not always be as exciting as young people would like it to be.
>
> (Associate professor, business)

Increased cost, increased answerability

An enlarged higher education system means a more expensive system and this enlarged system has as its end the service of business and industry as well as the development of knowledge for its own sake. No government will invest substantial and increasing amounts of money without ensuring universities are now accountable (Coaldrake 1998; Ramsden 1998). Employers, too, see themselves as influential stakeholders and, increasingly, look for influence into what is taught and how it is taught. University staff now work more closely and collaboratively with industry through the creation of joint consultative boards and committees (Candy *et al.* 1994) and there is a stream of employer satisfaction surveys (see, for instance, the DEET *Business/Higher Education Round Table Report 1991*). One staff member expressed his concern thus:

> At times, it seems we are here to just attend to concerns of employers and government. Our expertise concerning what might be important to teach is dismissed as being of little relevance. The trendy words are graduate attributes and employable skills and I wonder what happened to the university I used to know and love because it certainly isn't what we have now. There must be out there a group of students who are like we were, who like the idea of knowledge and knowing for its own sake, who want to know because there is a very basic human need to know and to learn. We do them, and I believe our society, a great disservice in attending only to the tinny tune of the uninformed employers who are concerned with quick profits rather than long-term development.
>
> (Associate professor, planning)

Students, likewise, can be seen as customers to be satisfied. When governments subsidise fees, then governments, themselves, are keen to ensure that the student experience is an effective and efficient one. When students pay their own fees there is even more resolve to ensure value for money. The new breed of student is a much more exacting taskmaster than his or her predecessor. She or he (there are now more women than men in undergraduate courses in both the UK and Australia) is less tolerant of poor teaching, inappropriate curricula or haphazard administration and this dissatisfaction does not rest with a low score on an evaluation questionnaire. It translates into poor scores on a whole range of performance measures, league tables and market-survey guides. This, ultimately, affects funding of courses and the livelihood of those associated with them as seen in this comment:

> There's this thing called educational negligence. It means that when students are not happy with what they are learning in their courses they take you, or the university, to court. It means we are now very cautious about what we teach and what we claim and what we try out . . . and this has some significant negatives because I always liked teaching to be as much a mystery tour as an express train. Now there is no discovering of pleasant byways. It's just straight through the main content in the most efficient way we can.
>
> (Associate professor, architecture)

Teaching more flexibly

Teaching more students and teaching students who are aware of their right to satisfactory service means that the focus of teaching has shifted away from the needs of the teacher to those of the student – in theory at least. So, at the same time as the contemporary university teacher has to attend to the needs of more and more varied students and more vocational courses, they are also being asked to attend to more flexible ways of teaching. They are being asked to take advantage of the flexibility of e-mail tutorials and broadcast lectures (Coaldrake 1998; Ramsden 1998). They are being encouraged to explore the resources available in multi-media packages and through a range of Web-sites. They are expected to take account of the possibilities of computer programs for students and, of course, they are being encouraged to consider the potential of linking with other classrooms worldwide via an interactive video classroom. And, whilst they are trying out these new ways of teaching in these new courses with these new students, they are also attending to new demands for accountability as expressed here:

> I dislike technology, but I know I will have to master this fear if I want to stay up with the job. I can see the advantages but I would like a sheltered environment to get used to new ways. I presently teach two large first-year classes. Six hours of teaching to 280 students. The rest of my teaching is second-year classes of around 60 students. I feel pressure in all of this contact time. There's no safe ground or friendly small groups to try something out.
>
> (Lecturer, nursing)

Internationalization

Internationalization of higher education is not just about Western nations providing education for less-developed nations and, consequently, increasing revenue. Underpinning the notion of internationalization is the idea of developing a shared understanding of cultures and politics and markets. Participants have the opportunity to teach and to learn from each other and, ultimately, to benefit socially, educationally and financially. The governments of some nations, most usually developing ones, tap into educational expertise offered worldwide. Universities make available learning experiences which offer relevant knowledge and expertise and which earn fees and closer economic and social ties for themselves and the nation.

Few universities can afford to turn a blind eye to the opportunities of immediate revenue and longer-term social and cultural benefits and nor should they – but few university teachers can cope unsupported with the complex challenges these opportunities present. Those working in Australasia, where East meets West, are particularly challenged. These challenges are not limited to teaching students with foreign cultures and foreign languages, though this is where much concern is often expressed. These challenges involve developing curricula which are international; that is, curricula which provide opportunities for the two-way exchange of learning emphasized earlier.

Internationalization is about countries around the world learning from each other. For instance, in the case of business courses, the concept of taxation or management accounting is explored with reference to practice and meaning in a range of cultures and countries. It is not just a matter of less-developed countries learning about Western ways and views:

> The problem is not just in the students but in the curriculum. You have to rethink the subject to make it relevant to very different students. We have significant proportions of Chinese now, well how do you deal with a subject like accounting, when the culture is just so different. It's interesting but it's terrifying. They don't understand the free market economy, they don't understand English. Where do you start? We desperately need help with this. But all our universities see is the dollars that these students bring in, not the associated problems we face.
>
> (Professor, accounting)

> This year we had nine different nationalities represented. We have over 100 in this class and around 70 of them didn't have English as a first language. Around one-third are overseas full-fee paying students who are not familiar with the culture of learning dominant in our Western universities. At least ten have such problems with English that I have recommended that they take special lessons.
>
> (Senior lecturer, engineering)

These are just some of the challenges of the new academic work. In their publicity material, universities express enthusiasm for this new age of higher education (Ashenden and Milligan 1995). In their public addresses, senior university leaders are less sanguine but still hopeful (see, for instance, the observations of Peter Coaldrake 1998 and Roger Brown 1997). Academic leaders at the local level (for instance, head of department or unit), are often stressed by the challenges (Sarros *et al.* 1996). Those academic staff in non-leadership positions are also overwhelmed and often very dispirited as well (McInnis 1996).

Survey of academic staff

A hint at the ways in which academic staff experience the changed work has been given in the comments above. A more thorough analysis of responses follows.

Background

During 1995 and 1996, comments were collected from just over 160 members of academic staff in the UK and Australia about their experience of how academic work had changed over the previous five to ten years. The sample was essentially an opportunity sample: staff were contacted via telephone or e-mail in a range of universities where the author already had connections. The sample covered a range of institutions, including the very old and traditional, and the very new. It included staff at all levels of the profession. Respondents were asked to indicate their level of appointment and their leadership responsibilities, if any (see Table 2.1).

Staff were encouraged to consider both the positive and the negative aspects of their experiences. They needed little prompting to respond openly and at length. On the whole, the responses do not make happy reading. They paint a picture of despondency and frustration, with the – occasional – pocket of optimism.

Table 2.1 Breakdown of respondents to survey of academic staff ($n = 161$)

Level of appointment	*Leadership responsibility*	*n*
Senior leadership	Pro vice-chancellor/deputy vice-chancellor (all at professorial level)	3
	Dean (all at professorial level)	7
Leadership	Head of department	
	Professor	6
	Associate professor/reader	12
	Lecturer	1
	Head of course	
	Associate professor/reader	8
	Senior lecturer	6
Non-Leadership	Senior lecturer	65
	Lecturer	38
	Tutor/assistant lecturer	15

Table 2.2 Numbers of comments on teaching, research and administration

Topic	*Leaders*	*Non-leaders*	*Total comments*
Teaching	39	112	151
Research	12	42	54
Administration	39	105	144

Table 2.3 Areas of concern expressed in the survey of academic staff

Area of concern	*Leaders*	*Non-leaders*	*Total comments*
Consultation			
Lack of consultation	19 (44%)	89 (75%)	108
Consultation slows down decision-making	30 (70%)	–	30
Accountability			
Excessive	26 (60%)	94 (80%)	94
Excessive but has positive aspects	13 (30%)	40 (34%)	25
Vision Lack of it	28 (65%)	84 (72%)	112
Valuing people Not valued	33 (77%)	103 (88%)	136

Most of the comments collected in this survey related to teaching and to administration. It is not denied that there have been changes in research work and in staff's experience of research, but this was not the focus of the weight of comments. The breakdown of comments in terms of a focus on teaching, on research or on administration, is provided in Table 2.2.

There was, overall, very little variation between responses from the UK and Australia. The higher education systems in both countries have confronted similar challenges and staff appear to have responded in similar ways. The greatest variation in responses was between staff with leadership responsibilities and those without such responsibilities. About one-quarter of the sample described themselves as leaders. Mostly, this group comprised heads of department (19) though there was also a large cohort of course leaders or coordinators (14) that is, academic staff with overall responsibility for the three or four years of an undergraduate degree programme. There was a small cohort of seven deans and also included in the sample were three respondents at pro vice-chancellor level and above. These senior staff were a good deal more optimistic in their comments than were their more junior colleagues. Table 2.3 summarizes the responses of those in leadership and those in non-leadership positions. Clearly, this survey draws on a limited sample, but the results are sufficiently in line with results from larger studies of academic staff in Britain and Australia (Halsey 1992; McInnis 1996; Altbach 1997) to be considered seriously.

The analysis of this data focuses on four issues which were most emphasized by the staff. These issues appear to arise out of the changes to higher education as identified above. They are:

- consultation – or lack of it;
- accountability – or too much of it;
- vision – or lack of it;
- valuing people – or lack of it.

These are not the only concerns of staff, but they were the dominant ones. They were not only mentioned frequently, they were talked about with ardour. These are the issues which are explored below.

Consultation – or lack of it

- 75 per cent of staff in non-leadership positions commented on the lack of consultation;
- 44 per cent of leaders also commented that they were not consulted when important decisions were made by their own seniors;
- 70 per cent of leaders suggested consultation could slow down the decision-making processes.

A major concern of those outside of leadership positions was the lack of consultation on relevant and important issues. This concern was not absent from the comments of leaders with reference to their own, more senior, supervisors, but it was less of an issue. Leaders sometimes explained why they did not attend to the comments of staff, and they, typically, cited time constraints.

For those in non-leadership positions, there was a concern that the absence of debate on key issues was antipathetic to the sharing of information and open discussion at the heart of academic values and life:

> Debate and discussion is at the heart of our profession. It is what we value and it is what we base our teaching and our research upon. We share information and knowledge and insights. We work to convince our colleagues, or our students, that this or that is the case and this is the basis of learning. There cannot be healthy universities when decision-making within those universities embodies principles which are in opposition to those at the heart of good teaching, good scholarship and research.
>
> (Senior lecturer, humanities)

Another concern was that a lack of consultation often meant that bad, unworkable, decisions were made:

> The trouble with leaders taking decisions without discussion and consultation is that they are uninformed as to the consequences. In cutting the research centre, we cut connections with industry and considerable

potential for overseas collaboration and probably funding. That can't be in anyone's interest. It certainly is contrary to the university's proclaimed mission.

(Reader, psychology)

The following commentator showed himself familiar with the commonly-cited justification for a lack of consultation:

It is easy to make decisions when you don't have to pick up the consequences. I could make decisions which affected the life and work of senior people in this university very easily. I wouldn't give it a moment's thought – as they don't give the decisions which affect the life and work of us ordinary lecturers. When it is our work and our problems, naturally we want a say and one of the reasons we want a say is because we know something about what goes on and we actually believe we have something to offer.

(Lecturer, social science)

Some respondents were generous and commented on the pressures their leaders and supervisors faced:

I think it's a pity because it's not in character and this action will really split the department. There will be those who support her because she has a lot of friends but there will be those who think that this [taking a unilateral decision not to offer a number of elective subjects] is not on and will make a lot of ripples – with the Students' Union as well.

(Senior lecturer)

Leaders emphasized that if decisions were left to academic staff then no action would result. Academic staff preferred to play with ideas and debate rather than act. In a modern university, decisions have to be made and they have to be made quickly. The leaders surveyed believed that many staff were out of touch with where higher education was and with the new demands that it had to attend to:

I am constantly amazed at how out of touch my staff are with higher education in general. They are unsure about what are the demands of the university and what are the demands of the larger system and how the two relate. They are not even aware sometimes of how details relating to their own courses have changed. It's hard to treat them as responsible colleagues when they demonstrate they are so out of touch.

(Head of department, engineering)

A sizeable minority of leaders did themselves comment on the lack of consultation by their own supervisors, but they appeared less disturbed by it than those in non-leadership positions:

It's my department that'll be affected and I'm not even consulted when they change the profile. It seems as though those involved are the last to hear. It doesn't make sense but I no longer expect sensible decisions.

(Head of department, history)

> There are decisions made at the Deans' Forum which directly affect my course but I never hear anything, until it's all sewn up – and then I'm told. I know sharing information can be a delicate business. I'm a leader myself, but there are certainly times when it's appropriate and this was certainly one of them.
>
> (Course leader, leisure and tourism)

A minority of staff, both at leader and non-leader levels, made the important distinction between, on the one hand, getting consensus on a decision through debate and discussion and, on the other, consulting staff and then the leader taking responsibility for the decision:

> It is part of the role of the academic staff member that he or she will debate endlessly and the debating is the purpose, not the decision, and we do not live in a university where this is appropriate any more so I simply do not give my staff the opportunity. I sometimes consult, but I make it clear that I take decisions, not them. I do this and I encourage my heads to do the same.
>
> (Dean, faculty of law)

> I try to get debate on an issue even though I know there will be disagreement and unpleasantness. The point is to air the issue and to collect views. It is then my responsibility to make a decision.
>
> (Head of department, physics)

Overall, however, such distinctions were not well-articulated. Ordinary staff typically smarted as a result of a lack of consultation and leaders typically defended their actions by pointing to pressures to make quick decisions.

Accountability – or too much of it

- 80 per cent of staff in non-leadership positions complained that accountability measures were excessive;
- 34 per cent of staff in non-leadership positions acknowledged that although accountability was often excessive it could also be positive;
- 60 per cent of leaders complained that accountability was excessive;
- 30 per cent of leaders acknowledged some positive aspects of accountability.

More than any other aspect of their work, those in non-leadership roles complained about the increased accountability in their job. Their concern was not so much with accountability itself, but with the battery of accountability mechanisms which they saw as getting in the way of real work. Leaders, on the other hand, talked about accountability as an imposition but, typically, appeared less overwhelmed by it.

The following comments capture the concern of academic staff in non-leadership positions:

> If I demanded as many accountability measures of my students as are now demanded of us, they would not tolerate it . . . We are expected,

> on the one hand, to be responsible professionals and, on the other, to report on ourselves like high-school kids. I can do almost nothing without getting permission from a superior and everything I do I have to make a plan for and write a report on – to the extent that it's not worth doing anything anymore . . . and they claim they want us to be innovative and creative in this new climate!
>
> (Senior lecturer, mathematics)

> I have no argument with showing the government and the public that we know what we are doing and we do a decent job but what we are into at the moment is not about that, it's about accountability for accountability's sake. It is about tiny-minded bureaucrats who know or care nothing for the work of the university going power-mad with new and different ways of making us complete charts and forms and proformas.
>
> (Senior lecturer, humanities)

> I write plans and accountability statements like I used to write fairy stories for my kids. They are both works of fiction but the stories were more interesting. I do it to satisfy the need for documentation . . . And as long as it's documented nobody cares what actually happens.
>
> (Lecturer, English)

A few staff stressed that while there was such an emphasis on accountability, little reward went to those who tried to make sense of a seemingly senseless activity. The important thing was compliance with the scheme:

> Like most of my academic colleagues, I am not prepared to undertake meaningless tasks. I therefore redesigned the code-reporting scheme to make it useful to me and to other academic staff and potentially give the head feedback which would be more useful to her . . . I got no praise at all, simply a curt comment about a column missing. This is the level of input they are looking for. Rubbish in, rubbish out; that is what they are asking for and this is what they will get from most staff. I will continue to do something meaningful or do nothing at all.
>
> (Associate professor, business)

There was equal recognition by those in leadership positions that accountability was excessive but they appeared less overwhelmed by the resulting schemes and mechanisms:

> I spend around 75 per cent of my time in this job showing that I and the department can justify the money and trust we are given. I do not particularly like it, but that is the job and I do it. I understand it has to be done and I do not see anyone in my position not doing it.
>
> (Head of department, art and design)

There was, however, sometimes a touch of anger in the comments of leaders about the complaints they received about accountability from their staff:

> Everyone in the university is in the same position, from the Vice-Chancellor, to the first-year students; academic staff are no different to any one else in higher education. I do not understand why there is so much dissatisfaction about it.
>
> (Course leader, computer science)

> Staff expect students to be accountable; they expect me to be accountable. It seems they have a problem when it is them who are asked to be so.
>
> (Course leader, economics)

Some leaders suggested they saw aspects of the accountability mechanisms as helping to bring into line difficult staff:

> Every cloud has a silver lining. Dealing with these reports is a tedious and time-consuming process, but it does allow me to have the activities of certain members of staff documented and reported on. This is more than used to be possible and it is a considerable advantage in ensuring that people do what they are supposed to do.
>
> (Head of department, computer science)

Vision – or lack of it

- 65 per cent of leaders commented that senior leaders in the university showed inadequate or inappropriate vision or direction;
- 72 per cent of staff in non-leadership positions commented on the lack of vision or inappropriate vision of senior leaders.

Academic staff in leadership and non-leadership positions believe that senior staff, that is those at pro vice-chancellor level and above, are struggling with the task of plotting the new map for contemporary higher education. This was the issue over which both local leaders and ordinary academic staff were most united.

There was a shared concern that universities were often moving from crisis to crisis, doing what was expedient rather than working purposefully towards an identified and articulated coherent design. The following comment is typical of staff at the level of head of department:

> I'm to lead my staff somewhere, but there's no clear idea of where it is we're going. We need to stop the sham and realistically look at what is possible. I can't lead when I don't know where we're meant to be going.
>
> (Head of department, biology)

The following comment reflects a similar concern but is from an academic in a non-leadership position:

> These are challenging times . . . we all know the university is floundering. I don't pretend to have any answers, but then I'm not a vice-chancellor, or even a head of department. The university needs to do more leading

> from the front. It needs to sell us a realistic vision to follow, or to contribute to. We can't fight together because we've no idea precisely what it is we're fighting for.
>
> (Lecturer, political science)

Those staff outside of leadership positions were more likely to make comment about a perceived lack of concern or knowledge about 'chalkface' university activity. Often this related to the challenges of teaching:

> There is no overall picture of where we are going, or what higher education is about any more. We are expected to rally to this idea about cutting tutorials when everything we know about our discipline, everything we know about teaching it to students, tells us it's wrong.
>
> (Lecturer, health science)

Sometimes, however, concerns related to the pressure of work generally:

> I work about 60 hours a week. I teach a full load. I try to be enthusiastic and to run with things. I care about the students, I care about my job but I'm being expected to do even more and there's not even a clear direction of where the university is going any more. I have a young family and a pregnant wife. I am not prepared to take on any more. I will give the university as good as I get but, frankly, I do not believe I get very much at the moment, certainly we're not getting leadership.
>
> (Lecturer, chemistry)

A lack of belief that senior leaders themselves were seriously committed to some of the changes was clear in a number of responses. In the following quote, a course leader comments on an ultimatum he has received to have a new curriculum developed and accredited in four months. The university, in its guidelines on course development, insists that at least one full year should be given to the process:

> If they were serious, if this new curriculum was truly important, then we would be given time. I tell my students that worthwhile things take a bit longer. I'm telling the management that as well. I don't believe they mean to run with this or half the other things they demand . . . It is just a matter of kite-flying, of having another iron in the fire and, in the meantime, we have to do the work and suffer the consequences of ill-health, broken families and the rest.
>
> (Course leader, English literature)

There were only three senior leaders (pro vice-chancellor, or above) in our survey. It is inappropriate to make much of data from such a small sample. Given that it is this senior leadership group which is being criticized, however, it is appropriate to provide some response.

As we have already emphasized, the comments of this senior group, overall, were more positive than those of other groups. The first of the two extracts presented below, however, gives an indication of the pressure experienced by senior leaders:

> Academic staff want more freedom, deans want more power, the government want better results. And they are all looking to me to get it done or to blame when it's not done. I get a lot of the flack and that's what I'm paid for but in the end if I, if the university, cannot deliver we, all of us, at all levels will suffer nobody has anything – that is my responsibility but it's everybody's problem. We all must pull our weight.
>
> (Vice-chancellor)

This final comment emphasizes the mismatch between the problem as seen by this particular senior leader and the problem as seen by those in less senior positions, cited earlier:

> The challenge to the university is considerable. We are seeking out our traditional strengths and looking how to build on these and how to make these relevant in a modern society and economy. There is much room for ingenuity . . . We have ideas but they are not always palatable to staff who frankly don't want to change. The university has a future, but those in it who are unwilling to see it is a new future will probably not be part of it.
>
> (Deputy vice-chancellor)

Valuing people – or lack of it

- 88 per cent of those in non-leadership positions commented on feeling not valued;
- 77 per cent of leaders commented on feeling undervalued.

By far the most disturbing comments were those which revealed the low state of morale in many universities. The most extreme comments came from staff in non-leadership roles who talked about the feelings of disempowerment and despair they felt in the face of what they saw as unreasonable demands. Those in leadership roles may have been less despairing but comments about feeling undervalued and under pressure were present in more than three-quarters of cases.

Some of the comments from staff in non-leadership roles were angry, such as the following:

> I feel like the miller's daughter in the Rumpelstiltskin fairy story. Each day I do the impossible, I perform the miracle – but there's only greed for more, never gratitude for what I'm doing. I've covered up for those in responsible positions and I've got the university out of hot water on a few occasions but now I've had enough. I'm taking my case to the union and I'm also considering legal action.
>
> (Senior lecturer, social science)

Some were disbelieving:

> Our so-called leaders must know that the demands being made are unrealistic. We're here to help students to learn and that has been lost

> sight of. They pass a paper from one in-tray to another and it takes a second. The implications can cause us weeks of burning the midnight oil and the consequences . . . emotional strain, etc. are not given a moment's consideration.
>
> (Lecturer, business)

And some were simply tragic:

> I gave to my work what I should have given to my family. I now have no family . . . and I soon may have no job.
>
> (Lecturer, economics)

These were not isolated cases. Around 88 per cent of staff in non-leadership positions indicated that they felt undervalued in their work.

Those in leadership positions also felt undervalued but the concerns were different. Often the comments related to being trapped between the unreasonable demands of senior staff and the stubborn refusal on the part of the more junior staff to respond:

> It is an increasingly thankless task. I try to make an unpalatable message or task palatable to my staff and I get no thanks from anyone. Either my own leaders who feel I should make things happen quicker or my own staff who believe I should stand up for their position more.
>
> (Head of department, science)

> I am trapped between the unreasonable demands of senior staff and the stubborn refusal to respond of more junior staff. It is a most uncomfortable and thankless job I do.
>
> (Head of department, social science)

There was also, in the comments of some leaders, a rather more aggressive note. These leaders accepted that staff felt undervalued, as they did themselves, but suggested that this was the nature of the contemporary higher education environment and that it had to be lived with. 'Put up or shut up' was a phrase used on four separate occasions:

> The times are not good or easy in higher education . . . But it would be best for everyone if staff would accept things will not go back. We are going forward and there will be some pain in that but that is the way it is. Nothing is achieved by complaining.
>
> (Head of course, engineering)

The optimists

- 15 per cent of staff in non-leadership positions emphasized some positive aspect of their work;
- 18 per cent of staff in leadership positions made positive comments about their work.

I warned at the beginning of the chapter that, on the whole, these comments of academic staff do not make for contented reading. There were, however, some pockets of optimism. It is important not to neglect those things which staff found positive. Positive comments came from staff in both leadership and non-leadership groups. They largely emphasized opportunities and creative challenges recently faced:

> I have had to rethink a good deal of what I'm doing in teaching this subject. That was devastating at first but now I am excited by it and we are incorporating some state-of-the-art lab work in our teaching. The students are excited like never before and so are we.
>
> (Lecturer, science)

> I have been given the task of reorganizing the research supervision in this department and that is really an interesting challenge because we have not been very good at supporting our students until now and it is working extremely well and we are having good seminars and good progress and a good time ourselves.
>
> (Senior lecturer, social science)

> A year ago, I thought I had been handed a poisoned chalice [the head of a newly-formed department]. I believe we have come a long way in the year. We have made excellent links with the industry, we have made good links overseas, and I think the staff have had a taxing but satisfying year.
>
> (Head of department, business)

In a few instances, the positives staff emphasized related to the changing nature of higher education: the move to mass higher education; the growing internationalization of higher education; and the social benefits likely to emerge from these trends.

> I find teaching the big classes hard but, on the other hand, we are now giving a chance to students who would never have dreamed of going to university. I find that very satisfying.
>
> (Tutor, health science)

> We are teaching into a course in Asia, that is very interesting. It is very challenging but I think the benefits in terms of increased understanding between nations and people is most exciting.
>
> (Lecturer, business)

The survey results suggested that the optimism did, indeed, cluster together in pockets. In one or two areas, in a few universities, there were some people – leaders and those in non-leadership positions – who were working together, maintaining morale and finding satisfaction in their work. Not all was good; they had their negatives to offer, but not all was bleak either.

Conclusion

It is, of course, possible to suggest that this is a small survey and that a different sample would have revealed different things. It has to be acknowledged, however, that the present study is not alone in telling a predominantly dispirited tale. The work of Halsey (1992) in the UK and McInnis (1996) in Australia both emphasize the disheartened state of a large proportion of the academic workforce. Halsey talks of a 'humbled' workforce. McInnis emphasizes, amongst other things, the extent to which accountability so often gets in the way of real work. In the present study, it is clear that leaders and non-leaders see issues and problems differently and that there is an excess of bitterness and mutual blame. It is not a good foundation for growth and development.

The often-made remark of organizations and leaders that staff are their key resource and their major investment was never more true than it is in universities. Universities, perhaps more than any other type of organization, depend on the minds and the commitment of their staff. The intellectual and creative capital of the collective workforce of a university is portentous. Used effectively, it can do amazing deeds; misused, it will cost a lot and gain little. Clearly, at the moment, it is not being used to best effect.

Essentially, what is being asked of academic staff is that they change their ways of working and that they learn new ways of working. There is a good deal which has been written about learning, about learning in organizations, and about student learning and it seems that much of what has been written would be relevant to the problems presented here. In Chapters 3 and 4, I attend to what is salient in this literature.

3

Learning and Teaching in Higher Education

> The habit of active thought with freshness can only be generated by adequate freedom. Undiscriminating discipline defeats its own object by dulling the mind.
>
> (A.N. Whitehead)

Introduction

Chapter 2 presents a disheartening picture. Despite occasional pockets of optimism, academic staff appear overwhelmed with the enormity of the issues and challenges and – at all levels of the system – staff feel undervalued and overworked. This chapter presents some key ideas from research into student learning in higher education which can inform the situation. Aspects of this research will likely be familiar to many readers but this work needs to be revisited in the context of the confusion and disillusionment with academic work. It seems likely that there are parallels between students' experiences of learning and academic staff's experiences of working.

Approaches to learning

We begin with the question which is central to much discussion on learning – why is it that in any class, some students learn while others do not? This simple question was asked a generation ago by a team of researchers in Gothenburg. This early Swedish work (Marton and Säljö 1976; Dahlgren 1984) was significant because it helped us to think differently about the asking and the answering of this question. It helped us to ask a more heuristic question: 'Why do students make sense of the same task in different ways?' and it helped us to answer it, not just in terms of students learning more or less, but in terms of learning that was qualitatively different. It also helped us to see that there was a relation between the way students saw the task and made sense of it; the way they approached the task; and the quality of learning outcome that they achieved.

In the original Swedish experiment, students were set the task of reading an academic article relevant to their study and they were questioned as to what the article was about and also how they had gone about the reading task. One group of students worked to find out what it was that was being said in the article. They focused on finding out what the author meant and they considered the evidence he used to make the argument. When questioned, they were able to relate evidence to the conclusions. The outcome was that they got a complete picture of what the article was about.

A second group of students focused only on the text, on the words and on trying to remember things. They did not attempt to locate or to become engaged with the argument of the article; they did not try to see the place of the parts in making the arguments. The outcome, not surprisingly, was that these students did not have a complete picture of what the article was about.

What is significant in this work is the idea that there exists a relationship between the way a learner approaches a task, in this case reading a text, and the learning outcomes they achieve. If a learner approaches the text with the intention of seeking meaning, identifying the main arguments presented by the author or teacher and distinguishing this from the evidence presented to support the arguments, then they will likely work towards achieving the understanding intended by the teacher or text. If, on the other hand, they focus only on the text or teacher as a sort of container of information, with bits and pieces of things hung in there to be recalled as necessary, then they will likely take away from the exercise just bits and pieces of disjointed information. They will not pick up on the author's meaning because they do not see this as the purpose of the learning exercise.

So, this research showed us that some people approach a learning task differently, but the question remained – 'Why is this?' A partial answer came through another important Gothenburg study (Säljö 1979). This study suggested that people learn differently because they actually think of, that is conceive of, what learning is quite differently.

Roger Säljö interviewed students about what they thought learning was and he found five qualitatively different ways of making sense of learning in an academic context:

- Learning as a quantitative increase in knowledge; that is, learning as 'knowing a lot'.
- Learning as memorizing; that is, learning as storing information that can be reproduced.
- Learning as applying, skills or information.
- Learning as understanding, making sense or abstracting meaning.
- Learning as interpreting and understanding something in a different way. Learning involves comprehending the world by reinterpreting knowledge.

In 1993, a further study by Marton *et al.* identified an additional conception of learning:

- Learning as changing as a person. Here, learning involves not just seeing the world differently but seeing one's own position in the world differently.

Each of these conceptions of learning is more complex than the previous one, and can be seen to incorporate the previous one. For instance, the first conception, 'learning as knowing a lot', is contained within the second conception, 'learning as recalling and reproducing'. The third conception, 'learning as applying facts or skills' embodies the previous two and so on.

This idea that lower-order conceptions nestle within higher-order conceptions is an important one in much of the student learning research but it is not one explored here (for a fuller discussion, see Marton and Booth 1997). Here, we focus on another important idea: that the conceptions of learning highlighted above can be readily divided into two groups. The first group contains the first three conceptions and, within this grouping, learning is tied to the particular circumstances of a task. Both what is to be learned and how it is learned are *not* seen as an issue or problem. Learning just involves taking in something new and adding it to what is already known; to quote one student:

> Well . . . you just learn it, just get in your head what's there and then just reproduce or represent that.
>
> (First-year law student)

Within the second grouping containing the last three conceptions listed above, however, what has to be known and learned is not so clear cut. Learning does not just relate to the context in which the problem or issue is found. It has to go beyond this into other aspects of life. Meaning has to be tested in different circumstances and learning might well involve changes in existing understanding. Another law student illustrates this:

> I like to try to get a grasp of the overall meaning. When I read I try first of all to think why is this important, what is the big message, why has it been chosen. I actually think of it in terms of a series of real-life problems. I find I probably change my mind about that two or three times when I'm going over it. I finally go with something and then look at the case in the light of that and other cases as well. Sometimes I completely change my idea of what it's all about but I might well change my mind again when I have a tute [tutorial] or talk to someone.
>
> (First-year law student)

This division between the first three and the final three conceptions is the division between a surface and a deep approach to learning. A surface approach is tied to what is given in a specific learning situation, a text or problem. The focus is on providing an answer in terms of the specific instance. A deep approach, however, goes beyond the given and looks to see the larger issues represented by a particular problem. The relationship between approaches to learning and conceptions of learning can be represented as in Table 3.1. The relationship of conception to approach is clearly a close one. The two things might be described as two sides of the same coin.

Table 3.1 Summary of the relationship between conceptions of and approaches to learning

Surface approach	
• Learning as a quantitative increase in knowledge	
• Learning as memorizing and reproducing	
• Learning as applying facts, skills and methods	
Deep approach	
• Learning as understanding	
• Learning as seeing something in a different way	
• Learning as changing as a person	

To summarize the argument so far – this early student learning research established the relation between a student's conception of learning and that student's approach to learning, on the one hand, and the quality of the outcome achieved on the other. From a practical teaching and learning perspective, it becomes clear that those students who approach a task by seeking the meaning intended by the author or teacher, and weighing given evidence to test that meaning, will more likely understand what the text or teacher is trying to tell. That students grasp the message we want them to hear is clearly important to us as university teachers.

The original experiment concerning student approaches to learning tasks and the resulting outcomes focused on the reading of an academic article. Subsequent investigations extended the work to include the way students undertake a range of academic tasks in different contexts and disciplines; for instance, how students work on problem solving in maths and science (Laurillard 1984) and how they experience learning in lectures in business students (Hodgson 1984). In all cases, it was possible to identify a relation between approach to the task and the quality of the outcome. Laurillard's study of problem solving emphasized the difference between the content of the problem and the problem in context. She found that some students focused on the problem in context, in the larger setting of the subject matter. These students actively engaged in thinking about the subject matter and in working with the relations within the problem. Doing the problem helped them to develop insight into the subject as a whole, for example:

> I suppose I'm trying to image what the experiment is talking about, in a physical sense, sort of get a picture of what it's about. This one says an ultra-violet lamp emits one watt of power; it says calculate the energy falling on a square centimetre per second. I'm just thinking of the light and the way it spreads out, so therefore I know it's the inverse square law.
>
> (Laurillard 1984: 136)

There were clear parallels between students who worked in these ways, focusing on the problem in context, and those students who Marton and Säljö (1976) described as taking deep approaches when making sense of a text.

Laurillard (1984) found that those students who focused on the content of the problem could equally be likened to those students who adopted surface approaches in the earlier Gothenburg work. These students worked only to recognize the type of problem and then to fix it with a formula. Their learning was, consequently, limited to working through formulas:

> It practically tells you what equation to use. You just have to bash the numbers out . . . There's not really any thinking. You just need to know what you need to solve the problem.
>
> (Laurillard 1984: 136)

Laurillard comments that if the student responds to the problem in context rather than the content of the problem, a qualitatively inferior outcome learning is inevitable.

Hodgson (1984) explored the way business studies students engaged with lectures. She developed the idea of extrinsic and intrinsic relevance, which again paralleled deep and surface approaches. Those students who sought and found intrinsic relevance attempted to make personal meaning of the taught content. They explored the comments of lecturers for relevance and when they failed to find it they asked questions, both of the lecturer and of other students until they found some meaning. Students who sought only extrinsic relevance were only concerned to get material down. They were not concerned about seeing the meaning or relevance of the material.

These two studies were a part of a body of early work which helped to extend the deep/surface distinction into a range of disciplines and learning situations. These studies, like the hundreds of studies which have followed, verified the salience of the deep/surface distinction across learning tasks and disciplines and reinforced the links between approaches to learning and the quality of learning outcome.

Misunderstanding of deep and surface approaches

The idea of deep and surface approaches to learning is, at one level, common sense. Both as teachers, and as learners, we understand the difference between engaging in the issues and challenges a task presents and in doing the minimum as defined by the requirements of the specific task, but this deceptively simple and useful distinction is often misunderstood.

One of the most common misunderstandings is that deep and surface approaches are of more or less relevance in different disciplines. The common misunderstanding is that a concern about details is related to surface approaches and a concern with overall ideas is related to deep approaches. In science and related fields, it is necessary to learn the detail; therefore surface approaches are sometimes seen to be essential. In the humanities and arts areas, however, deep approaches are sometimes argued to be more appropriate because the focus of learning is on major ideas rather than the details.

The point to be made is that *all* learning – be it in the sciences or in the humanities – requires the relating of argument and evidence or major concept and detail. Surface approaches might mean just memorizing or listing a series of related facts or they might mean listing a number of unsupported arguments. Students adopting deep approaches will always have the intention of working to make meaning through the manipulation of more detailed information.

Perhaps an even more common misunderstanding of the deep and surface distinction is that the approach a student adopts is seen to be a characteristic of the student themselves. Approach is here confused with another idea which is that we, as individuals, display some relatively consistent learning traits or styles (for a fuller discussion, for instance, see Entwistle and Wilson 1977). It may be useful at different times to focus on a more consistent learning style or characteristics, but approaches to learning are not like this. There are no deep learners and surface learners; students adopt different approaches in different circumstances.

The science students interviewed in the Laurillard study, discussed above, demonstrate how the same student can adopt different approaches in different circumstances. In one situation, a particular student says:

> I suppose I'm trying to imagine what the experiment is talking about, in a physical sense, sort of get a picture of what it's about. This one says an ultra-violet lamp emits one watt of power; it says calculate the energy falling on a square centimetre per second. I'm just thinking of the light and the way it spreads out, so therefore I know it's the inverse square law.

In another context, the same student observes:

> Formulae. You just have to go into the exam with as many formulae as possible. So you learn those parrot-fashion. And techniques involved in maths. I remember these just sort of one day.

Likewise, a second student from the same study, when talking about working in one context, observes:

> It's an operation research exercise, a programme to find a minimum point on a curve. First I had to decide on the criteria of how to approach it, then drew up a flow diagram and checked through each stage. You have to think about it and understand it first. I used my knowledge of OR design of starting with one point, testing it and judging the next move. I chose this problem because it was more applied, more realistic.

In another context, he comments:

> I knew how I'd do it from looking at it . . . it practically tells you what equation to use. You just have to bash the numbers out.

What is being emphasized here is that students will perceive different contexts and situations as requiring different approaches. Students are not deep or surface learners; rather, they adopt the approach they see to be appropriate in the circumstances. This issue is the focus of the next section.

The context of learning

The argument, so far, has been that there is a relation between the way students conceive of, and approach, a task and the learning outcome they achieve. We now extend this argument further by suggesting a relation between the way students perceive of the context in which they learn, the way they approach the learning task and the subsequent learning outcome. This relationship can be represented as follows:

Context ———— Conception/Approach ———— Outcome

The research into student learning described above was novel because it focused on students' experience of learning, not teachers' or researchers' experiences. It studied real learning tasks usually in the natural setting of the classroom or lecture theatre. It did not study artificially-created learning tasks in an experimental situation. Part of the reason for studying learning in a natural setting was to consider what it was within that setting that influenced learning.

The work of Ramsden and Entwistle (1981) is of particular significance when we look at the way context influences approach and outcome. An extensive, national study of UK university students was undertaken which clearly demonstrated the link between the context in which students learn, the approach they adopt and the outcomes which they achieve. The study involved the interviewing of students about their studying and the contexts in which they studied. It also involved the development of the Course Perceptions Questionnaire, ultimately the Course Experience Questionnaire (CEQ) which is now a major international measurement of student learning at the level of the subject or course. (A full and recent account of the development of this instrument is to be found in Wilson *et al.* 1997.) Through the interviews, it was discovered that students who reported using deep approaches were more likely to perceive the course as one in which the goals of the course, or subject were clear, the teaching was effective (with support and feedback from staff) and in which there were opportunities to demonstrate some independence in studying. These students were also likely to describe their learning, overall, as very satisfying.

Students who responded using surface approaches, in contrast, spoke of an excessive workload in the course, and inappropriate assessment regime (which tested the ability to reproduce facts and ideas rather than to interrogate and investigate relations within a subject) and of poor feedback on progress. These students were much more likely to express negative attitudes to their studies. The table created by Ramsden (1992: 81) offers a useful summary. It outlines the characteristics of the context of learning associated with deep and surface approaches.

Surface approaches are encouraged by:

- Assessment methods emphasizing recall or the application of trivial procedural knowledge.
- Assessment methods that create anxiety.
- Cynical or conflicting messages about rewards.
- An excessive amount of material in the curriculum.
- Poor or absent feedback on progress.
- Lack of independence in studying.
- Lack of interest in, and background knowledge of, the subject matter.
- Previous experience of educational settings that encourage these approaches.

Deep approaches are encouraged by:

- Teaching and assessment methods that foster active and long-term engagement with learning tasks.
- Stimulating and considerate teaching, especially teaching which demonstrates the lecturer's personal commitment to the subject matter and stresses its meaning and relevance to students.
- Clearly stated academic expectations.
- Opportunities to exercise responsible choice in the method and content of study.
- Interest in, and background knowledge of, the subject matter.
- Previous experience of educational settings that encourage these approaches.

Learning scales

This important study found what it was about teaching which made a difference to the way students learned. The study established a relation between students' perceptions of key aspects of the context in which teaching and learning took place and student approaches to learning. These key aspects of the learning context were identified through a series of interviews, but were subsequently developed into questions and scales on the Course Perceptions Questionnaire, later the Course Experience Questionnaire (Wilson *et al.* 1997). Over nearly two decades, these scales and questions have been found to be generally applicable across different higher education systems and disciplines.

If we want to know more about how the context effects student learning it is useful to explore each of the five scales: *Good Teaching; Appropriate Assessment; Clear Goals; Independence*; and *Appropriate Workload.* Student comments are used to illustrate the points made in this exploration. These student comments have been collected by a range of university teachers undertaking a qualification in university teaching and learning in the author's own university. Early in their course, these academic staff members are asked to explore the experiences of their own students' learning through interview. The comments have been selected from a range of disciplines to illustrate the connection students themselves make between the teaching context, their approach to learning and the sort of learning outcomes they achieve.

Good Teaching

What 'good teaching' involves can be debated endlessly, but when we ask students about their experiences of good teaching they express little doubt as to what it is. They repeatedly emphasize the same qualities:

- *enthusiasm* for and *knowledge* of the subject matter;
- regular and timely *feedback* for students; and
- a capacity to engage students with the mystery and importance of key ideas; but equally
- be able to give a *clear explanation* of these ideas.

These are the qualities picked up in the Good Teaching scale of the CEQ and are explored below with the help of student comment.

Enthusiasm and knowledge We begin with the often repeated idea (see for instance, Rowntree 1977; Eble 1988; Marton and Booth 1997) that it is the teacher who wraps up key issues and knowledge into stories and problems which students want to explore, who helps students to learn and to commit to learning:

> I believe that the reason I am in this class is because in Year 10 I had a very good English teacher, until that time I'd not liked English much really. But she just taught me to see things I'd never seen. I realised I'd done all my reading with my eyes closed till then. I've had bad teaching since, but through that woman I learned to see so much in the narratives and to get a great deal out of it both in terms of understanding the discipline of English and how writers communicate but also in my personal life that won't die no matter how much bad teaching I get now.
>
> (First-year arts student)

> I didn't particularly look forward to doing business. I just thought it would be useful and there's certainly lots that's a bit tedious but the subjects on tax reform, unlikely though it may seem, have really got me into them. I'm actually going to do my professional practice in a firm of tax consultants . . . I think I probably want to go that way with my career. I know it sounds unlikely, but somehow it's the way John and the team [lecturer and teaching team] present the stuff and help you to see the challenges and interest inherent in the subject so you can easily get more complex responses to the problems. In a lot of subjects you get the feeling the teaching staff are as bored as you are.
>
> (Second-year business studies student)

The above testimony of students concerning enthusiasm is compelling.

Clear explanation Enthusiasm and knowledge, however, are by no means enough. There has to be clear explanation. Sometimes teachers use diagrams or models, sometimes they use anecdotes, sometimes they use role-play or experience. Numerous books on teaching advocate skills and techniques to help teachers explain (for instance, Habeshaw *et al.* 1984; Eble 1988). It does not matter what is used, but it does matter that the students are helped to understand what is being said and the technique itself does not become over dominant. The following comments from students illustrate this point:

> He spends ages giving anecdotes about his professional experience and I suppose they're supposed to prove some point and explain something – but I don't know what. I never get the point of it.
>
> (Second-year business student)

> We have these role-plays and they're good fun, but I'm not at all sure what we learn out of them. I wish it was made clearer what the point was. What we were supposed to learn as a result.
>
> (First-year nursing student)

The experience of the following student, this time in statistics, is very different:

> I never was very good at maths, so I wasn't looking forward to statistics. I was really impressed with the way Dr F. went about it. Every topic or idea had heaps of explanation and examples, and it wasn't just the usual stuff; he really tried to get examples or to draw images that the class or the ones like me who had difficulty could relate to.
>
> (First-year psychology student)

Feedback The third aspect of the good teaching scale is feedback. Put simply, students need to know how they are doing before it is too late to do much about it. One of the biggest concerns of students is that they receive inadequate feedback; often the first piece of feedback they get is when they fail an exam or do badly in a major assignment. Giving feedback on how students are progressing is just as important as providing new information, but rarely attended to with the same vigour. This sort of on-going feedback is called formative assessment or feedback. It directs, corrects and realigns the day-to-day learning of students and, as the comments from students below show, it has a powerful effect on their learning:

> The whole point of the teaching is to help us learn but we really don't get much feedback along the way. We're told stuff, but there's not much opportunity to check if you see it right. You spend a lot of time trying to check out if what you think is the case actually is the case. You ask questions but getting straight answers back is frankly quite rare. I would do more real work if I didn't spend so much time checking out what I thought was wanted.
>
> (First-year arts student)

> I find the feedback we get in tutes [tutorials] very useful. You are drawn out about what you think or how you understand a topic and then this is discussed and considered and alternative ideas are put forward – and you can see your ideas sharpening up and falling into shape. It's this sort of teaching which is really useful. It's not just

> aimless discussion. The discussion is kept on track and informed and you really move your ideas. I wish there was more of this sort of thing in my other classes.
>
> (Third-year business studies student)

In summary, our students have little hesitation in telling us how they experience teaching and what good teaching looks like to them. Time and again they emphasize the trinity of the qualities which comprise the 'good teaching scale': *enthusiasm, clear explanation* and *timely feedback.*

Appropriate Assessment

The Appropriate Assessment scale is most important, for assessment, more than anything else in formal education, drives learning. We are told so by those who write about assessment and by the students who experience it. Yet, this is the area which students find the least satisfactory. They report more dissatisfaction on this scale (nationally in Australia) than on any other of the CEQ scales (Ramsden 1998). The biggest challenge with assessment is to ensure that what is assessed is that which has to be known. Sometimes, it is tempting to assess predominantly the surface signs of the subject or discipline, those things which can be assessed easily and marked quickly. For instance: 'List five features of good environmental planning.' It may be necessary for students to know these things, but such things would not be the extent of desirable knowledge at higher education level. More in-depth conceptual knowing in disciplines or professions involves comprehension of complex relations in variable situations. It is hard to ask questions which probe the subtle complexities of this type of knowing and just as hard to mark them. Devising good assessment is, undoubtedly, one of the most difficult aspects of teaching – but given that the de facto curriculum becomes that which is assessed, it is vital to work at it. The question about good environmental planning above, for instance, might be rephrased as: 'Consider the Bonvale New Town Development; show how principles of good environmental planning were applied, or ignored, and how they work, or fail to work, in this particular case.' Sometimes teachers complain they have no time to mark such complex answers. Rowntree (1977) points out that assessment is teaching. If we have no time for sound assessment, we might as well give up on teaching altogether.

The comments below show that students are quick to pick up the messages given by the assessment:

> I think there's a lot you could do with this . . . but we've only got to write 200 words on four topics so I haven't bothered. I've just got a fairly general understanding of about half a dozen of the main lesson topics so I'm pretty sure to cover the exam paper.
>
> (Second-year social science student)

> We have this tutor who's really good and you get a real good understanding of what's happening and I think it would be good if the

> lecturers, if they went into that more and used models and told stories but then other students don't support this because in the end you've just got to get through the exam and for the exam you've just got to be able to do the maths.
>
> (Second-year electrical engineering student)

> This was a new subject we were told that we'd have to be able to really understand this stuff and these theories and give examples and explain what they meant in novel situations . . . But the exam, it wasn't like that at all. It wanted some very specific stuff and nobody had learned that sort of detail . . . Well, I'll be more careful next time. I'll make sure I see examples of the sort of stuff they give us.
>
> (First-year environmental science student)

In summary, students experience assessment as a powerful force directing their learning. In seeking the truth about our assessments, we would do well to attend to what students say.

Clear Goals

When students fail to learn, it is often because they are unclear about what they need to know. There are two related issues here. First, students might believe that teachers have not made the requirements clear and, secondly, they might believe that teachers have made the requirements clear, but they are disbelieving that what they are told is really the case.

If we consider the first scenario, as university teachers, we know that we can present information to students many times, but they will not necessarily know what we have told them – and, at one level, this is not surprising because, as has been emphasized before, teaching is not telling, it is rather about the students' receiving and making sense of the information.

Let us consider the following two comments and bear in mind, as we do so, that both of these students had the assignment requirements laid out in a course handbook and both had at least one face-to-face session concerning the assignment:

> The biggest thing is that I don't know what is expected in this essay. The essay questions are all so vague and when you ask questions about it the answers are equally vague. It seems as though they want us to surprise them . . . but I know that really they have quite set ideas about what's good and what's not and the trick is to find that out. That's what we're all working on at the moment. Once I know what is wanted then I can get on with trying to give it.
>
> (Second-year social science student)

> There's this assignment which is a real practical problem. There's plenty of stuff written about what's wanted, but I'm not sure what that means in terms of what I do. I would really like to see an example of previous assignments to get a really good idea.
>
> (Second-year chemistry student)

It seems we cannot tell our students too much, or too often, about what we are looking for from them and how we want them to demonstrate their knowing.

The second situation concerning lack of clarity is when students are aware that they have been given advice and requirements; at one level, they think they understand, but, at another level, they are disbelieving that the advice is sound for it appears to be at odds with their expectations of what might be required. The following student makes the point:

> I know how to solve the problems – according to the template, but I had never been asked to do more than that so, when I was told that I would have to actually look at the company in the light of the financial projection, I didn't really take notice. I suppose I wasn't really tuned in to what that really meant because I thought I'd done this sort of thing before so often.
>
> (Second-year accounting student)

The disbelief of the following student takes a different form:

> The trouble is that if you look at the handbook it says that this project should demonstrate creativity and innovation. But when you look at what we've been taught, it's the opposite . . . I'm not sure that creative and innovative is really what's wanted here. It just doesn't fit.
>
> (Second-year engineering student)

It is important to balance the picture with some more positive student comment:

> It's very hard to know what's expected of you when you first come to university . . . I've been lucky because Dr B. is the lecturer for the subject and he doesn't seem to mind how often you ask him about it. So, in the beginning, I was not sure that the environmental issues were at all relevant to engineering and now I can see that they are exactly so – and he has helped me to see that, so by the end of the semester, I am really getting a clear idea of how to tackle the major assignment and what this subject is whereas, in other subjects, that is not the case.
>
> (First-year engineering student)

Overall, we need to ensure that our students are clear about the expectations and goals we impose. They need to know what they are and believe that they are salient.

Independence

At first sight, it seems an anomaly that students should require both clear goals and independence but it is the case. Students need guidance to know what it will be profitable for them to focus on – but they also need space and support to make imaginative connections and explorations. Learning is a creative and an imaginative act. Guidance is essential but too much control will undoubtedly result in suffocation. The following comments of students help us to understand the way they see it:

> I have to feel confident that I'm on the right track and I've got that confirmed by the lecturer – then I can work quite independently and I usually do well because I've brought out stuff which wouldn't be generally known or focused on.
>
> (Second-year social science student)

> This year you are given more space in an assignment and this means you can be more creative, but you have to work within boundaries and sometimes these are explicit in the assignment and if they're not then you've got to check what they are because there will be parameters to work within.
>
> (Second-year civil engineering student)

> We work in teams and we get some real excitement out of it. We come up with much more creative solutions this way, but it's also good because working in the team you're kept in line. You don't go off too much on a tangent. There's somebody there who brings you back to the purpose of the question.
>
> (Third-year maths student)

Bruner (1966) talks of teaching as being a temporary state with the aim of providing students with autonomy. Students who believe they have some independence in their learning are much more likely to engage in the task and achieve outcomes which they find satisfying. Such students describe driving themselves more and further because the questions they are raising are significant to them. The following student comments are revealing:

> I hate narrow set tasks I don't ever learn from them. I think this is why I'm doing so much better this year. There's much more freedom in second year . . . You're directed, of course, through the assignments but the responses you give are just expected to be more open.
>
> (Second-year psychology student)

> This course gives you a lot of freedom. You attend to what critics and writers have said and written but you then bring your own interpretations to that and that means you think a lot for yourself and spend a lot of time doing this. But you don't do it in a vacuum. You are working within the context of what you know the subject is and what you know is expected. That's part of what you are learning really, how to work within the discipline and then how to position your own thoughts and work within that.
>
> (Third-year arts student)

A.N. Whitehead is often quoted when the topic of independence in learning is raised. He is quoted at the beginning of this chapter, and his wisdom is most apt here:

> The habit of active thought with freshness can only be generated by adequate freedom . . . The university imparts information, but it imparts it imaginatively. This atmosphere of excitement, arising from imaginative consideration, transforms knowledge. A fact is no longer a bare fact: it is invested with all its possibilities.
>
> (Whitehead 1967: 139)

Appropriate Workload

'Excessive workload' can be explained with a reference to the author's own teaching.

The first subject I taught focused on Victorian poets. The experiences of my students were exactly the opposite of those of the last-quoted student. I spent weeks planning the subject and timetabled each precious minute of class time. I still found myself short of time, however, so I loaded the students with additional reading and exercises. I found that no-one did the additional work; in fact, very few appeared to do much work at all.

The evaluation questionnaires told me that I covered too much ground too quickly and gave too much work. The students' assessment tasks told me that the students did too little work, their responses were ill-informed and disheartening. For a while, it seemed an insolvable problem. How could I get students to do the work they had to do to learn what they had to know? It must be a question many teachers have asked.

Some two or three years later, when I taught a similar course, the preparation I undertook was of a different kind. I spent time thinking about what was the essence of the subject and what were the two or three things they had to know about Victorian poets to get a very basic understanding. This is what I subsequently focused on teaching. The consequence was that there was more class time to engage students – more time for them to reflect on the essentials, more time to compare their own reactions to writing and writers with those of recognized critics and with each other. The evaluation reports suggested students had appreciated the learning experience and assessment results showed they had learned far more than I had taught and far more than when, some years previously, I had frantically tried to cover more.

It is an important and difficult lesson to learn that more appropriate workloads for students will often mean we teach less – but that students will ultimately learn more! When teachers and students are panicked by an overloaded curriculum and heavy workloads, they are unlikely to feel they have the time to explore and to engage with topics. They are likely to feel pressured into just remembering and rote learning. Heavy workloads often mean that students memorize a lot for a short time – and understand very little:

> I have 22 hours of contact time. On top of that I have to write up lab notes and do weekly assignments in three subjects. I'm supposed to be working on a major project with a team and we're supposed to meet at

least twice a week for a couple of hours or so. I'm supposed to do work to bring to this group. I'm also supposed to do reading for my classes and prepare for end-of-term assessment. I live away from home and have to work to cover my expenses. I work three nights a week. I try to have a bit of social life and keep up with fitness training. Frankly, it's just impossible. Things aren't done properly because it's just not possible to do them properly. It's a bit of a vicious circle really because the more you skip on things the more you lose interest and the more you lose interest the less you do. I've not failed anything so far, but it's more good luck than anything else that I haven't.

(Second-year engineering student)

So, as was suggested above, the connection between heavy workload and learning is not a simple one. If students see the tasks they engage with as relevant and interesting then they rarely complain of workload. It is when students do not find tasks so engaging that work becomes a chore. We have to win the enthusiasm of students and enrol their commitment in a topic or subject before we can that they lose themselves in the work. Compare the following two student comments:

I just can't get interested in this topic and everything about it becomes a huge chore. I tried at first, because I thought this branch of chemistry would be interesting, but it was just so tedious the way it was taught and maybe, eventually, it will be interesting but there's no way I can get through all that tedious stuff to find the enlightenment, so I'll do the minimum and opt out as soon as possible.

(Second-year chemistry student)

I spend a lot of time on this subject. I just get involved with it. It doesn't seem a burden it is just what I want to do to answer the questions I have or to find out what I want to. I wouldn't say it was a heavy workload, you could get away doing much less but I don't want to.

(Second-year nursing student)

The final comment is from a student of commerce. This student distinguishes between two sorts of workloads, 'wallpaper workloads' which are constantly in the background keeping you busy but not inducing thought and 'prize packages' which you come across occasionally and which are savoured in the unwrapping and the exploring. They illustrate the argument concerning workload very well:

Most of the time it's just like wallpaper the workload. It's all around you. It's relentless. You do the stuff and it wears you down. You just do it because you have to, to keep up with things . . . But sometimes you get a real prize package. It's not like any of the rest. It stands out and it catches your imagination and you unpack it carefully and put a lot of thought and time into exploring it but you don't care about how long it takes because you learn from these sorts of assignments. It's not that it's a heavy workload, it's more that it makes you think really hard. It actually makes your work and your time at work worthwhile.

(Third-year commerce student)

The context of learning – a summary

If we want to know about our students' experiences of learning, we need only ask them – but we do need to know what to ask and also what to look for in the answers. We need a theory to guide us. The theory which underpins the student learning literature is the theory presented so far. This theory suggests that the context of learning, as experienced by the students, is related to the approach students take to their study and, subsequently, to the outcome they achieve. The way that context has been conceptualized here has been through the five key aspects or scales of the original Course Perception Questionnaire, later the Course Experience Questionnaire. This diagram helps to make these relationships clear:

The context of learning ———— approach ———— outcome

- good teaching;
- appropriate assessment;
- clear goals;
- independence;
- appropriate workload.

The parallels between students' experiences of formal learning and academic staff's experiences of their work as expressed in Chapter 2 must by now be apparent. There is, however, one last aspect which represents a final link in the arguments made so far and which needs to be explored.

Approaches to teaching

If students approach their learning in different ways then, perhaps, teachers approach their teaching in different ways – and if they do, then perhaps there is a relationship between the way teachers approach their teaching and the way students approach their learning and, ultimately, what students learn. These relations can be depicted diagrammatically:

Approach to teaching ———— Outcome of teaching

↕

Approach to learning ———— Outcome of learning

Out of the student learning research, there has now emerged a way of exploring teaching which parallels the work on student learning. This work focuses on the ways in which university teachers make sense of the act of teaching and the ways they consequently approach the teaching task. The approaches teachers take to their teaching have also been related to the approaches to learning and the learning outcomes of their students.

Keith Trigwell and Mike Prosser (1996a) have built on the work of other researchers (Martin and Balla 1991; Samuelowicz and Bain 1992) and found that teachers do think about and approach teaching in quite different ways. Trigwell and Prosser have identified five qualitatively-different approaches to teaching which have clear parallels with students' approaches to learning cited earlier. These approaches to teaching are:

- Approach A: Teacher-focused strategy, with the intention of transmitting information to students.
- Approach B: Teacher-focused strategy with the intention that students acquire the concepts of the discipline.
- Approach C: A teacher–student interaction strategy with the intention that students acquire the concepts of the discipline.
- Approach D: A student-focused strategy aimed at students developing their conceptions.
- Approach E: A student-focused strategy aimed at students changing their conceptions.

In brief, Trigwell and Prosser have identified variation along a dimension where, at one extreme, university teachers focus on their own role in the transmission of knowledge and, at the other extreme, they focus on the students and on changing the students' understanding. This work was undertaken in large first-year science classes, but other research has worked with students in different disciplines and found similar results.

Let us consider the comments of two teachers (designated as Teacher I and Teacher II) who would fit at either end of the continuum of teacher and student focus. These teachers were interviewed for another study on teachers' conceptions and approaches to teaching (Martin and Balla 1991). Both teachers are teachers of history and both are responding to a request to describe the teaching of a topic they were shortly to commence. First, we hear from Teacher I whose focus is on himself and his performance; the students are barely mentioned:

> I have a largish class of around 100 and so I make sure that I have all my notes and overheads in order and ready. I know what I have to say and I've usually checked I'll get everything in, but I make sure the important stuff comes in the first twenty minutes just in case anything goes seriously astray and I get side-tracked with questions or whatever. I have some printed notes but I don't give out these until after the lecture so they concentrate on me and what I'm saying. I talk for twenty minutes and then I have a lighter more anecdotal spell of about five minutes, to give them a bit of a rest and then I go on for a final fifteen minutes. I leave five minutes or so at the end for questions, but there aren't usually very many.
>
> (Teacher I)

If we consider what teaching is for this teacher, it is clearly a means to transmit information. That the students have to learn is not seen as a problem; the learning of the students is only distantly related to the act of teaching and is not at the heart of the teaching challenge. Getting timing right and content right is the challenge identified here. Let it be emphasized that this teacher was good at what he did. He delivered information effectively, but he was not a competent teacher for his focus was not on the purpose of teaching which is to improve student learning.

When we consider the following comments of Teacher II, we see that, in this case, the challenge of teaching is seen in a very different way:

> There's a trick in killing the myth and keeping alive the interest. There's a need to destroy arguments in order that students can rebuild their own. In the first two or three sessions I'm into the killing. It makes students question what they've probably thought was gospel. They might rise to defend it or they might join in in the slaughter – but either way they are engaging with the evidence. That's the aim. Once they engage they are on track with the learning. Once they engage then I start learning too – for we have a good deal to learn from our students.
>
> (Teacher II)

The task for students as represented by Teacher II is not just to learn more, but to change their way of seeing. There is also a learning task as well as a teaching task in there for the teacher. For this teacher, teaching involves learning from the students. This point has been picked up by a number of commentators in the area (Eble 1988; Ramsden 1992; Marton and Booth 1997).

A subsequent investigation by Trigwell *et al.* (in press) shows a clear relationship between a teacher's approach to teaching and their students' approaches to learning. So, when teachers do approach their teaching in ways similar to Teacher II, then students are more likely to approach their learning in ways which facilitate deeper learning outcomes. This is an important finding; it shows that good university teaching does make a difference.

The teaching environment

It might be assumed that if students' perceptions of the context in which they learn is significant in their learning, then teachers' perceptions of the context in which they teach might also be significant for teaching. Other recent work by Prosser and Trigwell (1997) has confirmed this; they have shown a link between teachers' perceptions of the context and their approach to teaching.

As has already been described, the Course Perceptions Questionnaire (subsequently developed into the Course Experience Questionnaire) taps into aspects of the context in which students learn. Prosser and Trigwell have done something similar for teaching and the context in which teaching takes place. Like Ramsden and Entwistle (1981), Prosser and Trigwell (1997) undertook interviews of teachers and, on the basis of these interviews, developed the Approaches to Teaching Questionnaire which measures teachers' perceptions of their teaching environment. When interviewed, teachers emphasized that the following things got in the way of their teaching: size of class; amount of material to be covered; the varied backgrounds and experiences of students. They also emphasized that control over what was taught and discussion and support of teaching from colleagues and supervisors acted positively on their perception of the environment.

Where teachers felt limited by the constraints mapped out above, they typically adopted information-transmission approaches. Where they felt less restrained, and, particularly where they experienced some freedom over what was taught and support for their teaching, then they were more likely to adopt student-centred approaches to their teaching. This finding needs some explanation for, at first sight, it appears to suggest that teachers who have light loads, small classes and students with high levels of prerequisite knowledge are the ones who are able to adopt student-centred approaches and help students achieve deep learning outcomes. The situation was, however, that all of the teachers interviewed worked in similar conditions. They all had large classes and their students had a wide range of backgrounds and they all taught to tightly documented, well-established curricula. But, for some of the teachers in the group, these conditions were seen as inhibiting factors while, for others, they were not seen as such. In the latter case, the teachers focused on developing understanding in the students and ways of engaging the students; these strategies were seen as part and parcel of the challenge of teaching.

To explain this further, let us return to the three-part model of the relation between context, approach and outcome, presented on page 41. Previously, the connections in one direction from context towards outcome have been emphasized. But the student-learning research emphasizes that learning is, in fact, 'relational', and that what we learn (outcome) cannot be divorced from how we learn (approach) and that both of these things have to be seen in terms of the context in which learning takes place (Ramsden 1992; Biggs 1996b; Marton and Booth 1997). It is inappropriate to see the model as a causal one; it suggests interactions which can affect each other in any direction. So, the way a task is approached can influence a teacher's or a student's perception of the context, just as their perception of the context can influence their approach.

An example is useful here, but first let us reiterate that we are focusing on *perceptions* of the context, that is, the ways in which teachers or students see and experience the context in which they teach and learn. Where teachers adopt information-transmission approaches to teaching and believe that their task is to cover all the relevant material then they will very often perceive their workload to be unmanageable because there will always be more relevant material to cover than can be got through. Where, however, teachers see their task as helping students to engage with key issues rather than to cover everything, then the task becomes more manageable just as it does for students who realize that they do not have to remember everything, they have to understand key issues.

By way of a second example, we emphasize another aspect of the Prosser and Trigwell (1997) findings: that interest in, and support of, teaching by colleagues and supervisors is important in maintaining enthusiasm and overcoming obstacles. The comments of one of the staff, who responded to the survey on academic work which is reported in Chapter 2, are relevant here. This teacher, a new teacher, was supported in such a way that she was able to change her understanding of teaching, feel less threatened by (and concerned about) the context in which she worked and, eventually, grew to enjoy her work:

> I was in my first year of teaching three years ago and, after a couple of months, I thought I would have to give up. I thought it would be easier than legal practice, now I've had my second child . . . it was certainly not. I couldn't cope with the preparation and with the marking and with the lack of even basic knowledge of the students. It was all just overwhelming . . . I was paired with a lovely colleague, Mandy, a mentor. She's the reason I, and my students, got through that first year. I just focused on all the content and all the students; I had 100 in my first-year class and I couldn't cope. I was working all hours at home and the kids were suffering and I was suffering and getting back into practice looked like a good option, but with Mandy's help I not only coped – I grew to enjoy it.
>
> (Lecturer, law)

Of course, the context can, and does, present us with conditions and situations which are limiting and serious. Certainly, the workloads of teachers, like the workloads of students, may be unmanageable, no matter how they are attended to. However, it is also the case that the support and enthusiasm of a colleague, supervisor or peer, and some control over what is taught can help us to forget the limitations and to focus on the central issue of our students' learning.

Conclusion: The lessons for contemporary academic work

A good deal of research has been presented in this chapter and it is useful to summarize and consolidate the main issues which have emerged.

Reference has been made to a model of learning which indicates a relation between the way students make sense of the context in which they learn, the way they approach a learning task and the learning outcomes they achieve. It has been argued that what this means in practice is that some learning which goes on in our classrooms is better than other learning.

Some leaning involves students changing their way of seeing and understanding a topic or phenomenon and changing, not in a haphazard way, but in ways which are consistent with knowledge and thinking in the area. Changing, in fact, in ways which academic staff and texts suggest they should change and which are consistent with the aims of the subject and the aims of higher education as a whole. Other students fail to learn or fail to learn what lecturers want them to learn. They learn isolated facts or topics but appear to have little idea how these fit together or how thought in the area is developing or how evidence relates to this.

The argument is that what learning is, what it involves, is seen in different ways by different students, in different contexts. Some students begin with the intention of making sense, of seeing the connections, the structure, the relation of evidence to argument. Other students see the task as simply involving a focusing on the surface aspects of the task, their intention being to satisfy the demands of the task rather than to engage with the issues. Perhaps, not surprisingly, different outcomes result from these different approaches and intentions. Where students intend to understand and engage, then they often do see what the lecturers expected or hoped they would see; where they do not have this intention, then, not surprisingly, they do not achieve the desired understanding. What is being described here is the distinction between deep and surface approaches to learning. We have seen that in different disciplines and tasks these approaches vary slightly, but, nevertheless, the deep/surface distinction appears relevant and generalizable across all learning at university level.

We know that the way students approach a task affects the quality of the learning outcome and we also know that students' perceptions of the context in which they learn affects the approach they take. The research cited above indicates that key aspects of this context are:

- *clear goals*, which make explicit precisely what is expected of students;
- *good teaching* which is enthusiastic, engages students in appealing problems and offers clear explanation and regular feedback;
- *assessment* which rewards deep understanding rather than surface responses and which reflects the issues and content emphasized through day-to-day teaching;
- *independence* which allows students the opportunity to explore topics and issues in ways which are relevant and significant for them; and finally, we know that
- *workload* is important and that this means not just avoiding too heavy a workload but also avoiding too trivial a workload – a workload which engages students rather than just merely busies them is what is required.

We also know from the research that there is a relation between the way teachers approach their work, the outcomes they achieve in terms of student learning and the way teachers perceive the context in which they work. In brief, where teachers see as manageable:

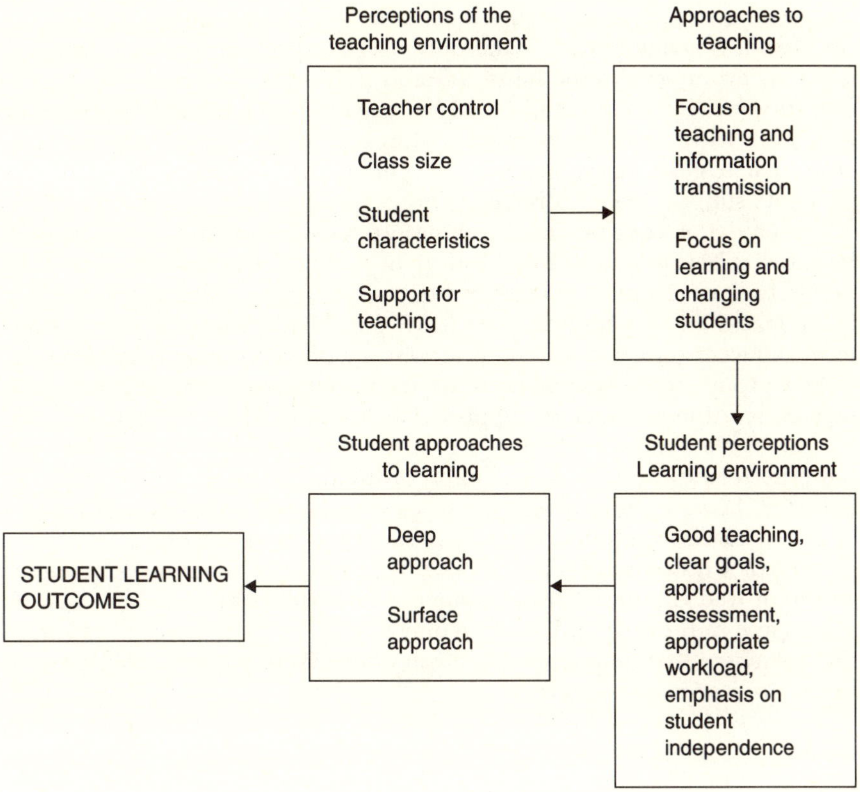

Figure 3.1 The relation between teachers' perceptions of the teaching environment and student learning outcomes

- the size of class they teach;
- the amount of material they cover; and the
- range of background and ability of students in their class;

and where they believe they:

- have some control over what is taught; and
- are supported in their teaching by colleagues and supervisors;
  then they are more likely to adopt student-centred approaches to teaching which are related to deep student learning outcome.

This is a long chain of relationships and it is presented diagrammatically in Figure 3.1.

From what has been emphasized about teaching and learning in this book so far, it is not difficult to see what supports teachers and students in their tasks of learning and teaching. Put very simply, they need some control over what they do and they also need some support and guidance in what they do.

Teaching is only a part of the work of an academic member of staff, but for most it is a vital part. It is the university's largest source of income and is clearly prominent in the minds of most staff – 138 of the 161 teachers in our survey specifically commented on teaching and related issues. If we look back to the comments from staff in the survey (see Chapter 2), it is clear that a good many believe they get neither adequate freedom nor adequate support and this is clearly not a healthy position to be in.

The model of learning (and teaching) we are working with in this chapter, however, is heuristic not causal. Failure in teaching and learning cannot be pulled back to teachers' perceptions of the context in which they teach and inadequacies in that context. It is clearly possible for students and teachers to work successfully in the most unsupporting of environments and they do.

As a group, recently-appointed academic staff experience extreme feelings of isolation and lack of support. Two studies (Boice 1992; Martin and Ramsden 1994) have both shown how these staff run the risk of, at best, underperforming and, at worst, simply giving up. Some small percentage of new staff, however, do not wait for support to be offered; they seek it out – and, as a result, often find themselves supported and successful.

There is a lesson to be learned here. We can wait a long time for support and improved circumstances to come our way. Meanwhile, our lives may be dismal and depressing and we have only one life. There is much wisdom in the old adage that help comes to those who help themselves. This point is further explored in Chapter 4.

4

Organizational Change and Learning Organizations

He that will not apply new remedies must expect new evils.

(Francis Bacon)

Introduction

The idea that organizations learn is a relatively new one. At the heart of the concept is the notion that to cope with rapid change, an organization must be adaptive. Stable structures and systems which once made organizations strong are now believed to contribute to their downfall. The organization which survives and thrives is the one that can change – the one that can learn. It is, of course, the people of the organization who change and learn and they use this learning to enable the organization to adapt and be responsive and it is the development of these people which is the focus of the literature on learning organizations.

As was seen in Chapter 2, universities are having to change; they are having to respond to a transformed environment. At the moment, however, universities appear unable to cope with the change and the rate of change they confront. Staff in universities are characterized by their leaders as being reluctant to adapt to the new conditions and the new environment while those in leadership positions are often characterized by staff as being unable to guide or to lead. The literature on the learning organizations was developed in the face of these very concerns in business and industry.

Perhaps the best known and most comprehensive work in the area of learning organizations is Peter Senge's book *The Fifth Discipline: The Art and Practice of the Learning Organisation* (1992). Senge explores and explains the qualities and understandings (the five disciplines) which staff must develop in order to move organizations towards 'learning organization' status. This chapter investigates these qualities and considers their relevance for those of us working in contemporary universities and colleges.

The learning organization

In the late 1980s, a world crisis in the business sector sent hundreds of firms into liquidation and a number of writers and researchers into rethinking their advice concerning the developing of efficient and effective organizations. Tom Peters and Robert Waterman were two such writers. In 1982, they had published *In Search of Excellence* in which 43 excellent companies were profiled. Five years later, two-thirds of those companies were facing trouble of varying degrees. Both authors agreed that their assumptions about excellence required some reworking and that part of that reworking had to be the acknowledgment that coping with change, or rather with the current unprecedented rate of change, had to be a major consideration. Peters' *Thriving on Chaos* (1988) and Waterman's *The Renewal Factor* (1987) were the books that heralded the surge of texts which have developed the idea that a successful organization is not a rigid, steadfast one, but one which develops and learns as it goes.

Senge (1992) was one of the first writers to use and to explore the concept 'learning organization'. It is Senge's work which is most drawn upon in this chapter. Senge's work is based on the idea that when organizations are large, people and circumstances generate behaviour and systems which prevent the organization and its people working effectively. The learning organization literature encourages a keener awareness of events external and internal to the organization and a more intense observation of, and reflection on, what happens. It discourages an oversimplified cause-and-effect analysis.

The five disciplines referred to in the title of Senge's book are:

- personal mastery;
- mental models;
- shared vision;
- team learning;
- systems thinking.

The fifth discipline is the critical mechanism by which the other four disciplines are integrated. The remainder of this chapter investigates each of Senge's disciplines, draws attention to other writers who have contributed to thinking in the area and flags the relevance of these ideas to contemporary academic work.

Personal mastery

An organization is as good as the people within it and the responsibility of turning the organization into a learning organization and staff into active contributors is shared by all staff. It is not a matter of there being inadequate leaders or inadequate staff – both leaders and staff have a part to play. Personal mastery, the first of Senge's disciplines, is the necessary starting-point for every member of the learning organization. It involves each individual having a vision of what they believe they can achieve and a faith in their capacity to work towards this, no matter how restricting and frustrating the environment. Of course, there will be things that get in the way; this is the nature of life and social systems, but the response should be one of finding ways of working in the face of adversity, rather than one of cataloguing and complaining about the problems.

Let us return to the things which impede personal mastery. There is a good deal of literature which focuses on impediments to effective work in organizations (Weber 1947; Bennis 1989; Drucker 1990). This literature is important and is often cited in the learning organization literature. It is cited because it helps us to know what to avoid and the challenges we are likely to confront. It is not cited to encourage inactivity in the face of challenges.

Dr W. Edwards Deming (1988), best known for his work on the development of quality systems and outcomes in organization, has catalogued the ways in which organizations build up an armoury of tools which discourage staff from learning and contributing their best. He particularly emphasizes the following three points:

- the excessive paper work;
- the attitudes of some staff which denigrate the enthusiasm and commitment of colleagues;
- and the way in which staff are put down when they attempt to contribute or critique anything not in line with official policy.

These points will no doubt ring true with a good many academic staff. Indeed, the following comment is one received in the survey of academic staff:

> In my department, over the past three or four years, there has developed this ethos of cynicism and minimal compliance . . . I hate it because to me it seems it's the students who suffer and when it comes to the bottom line, they're the ones we're here for . . . But anyone who shows some enthusiasm is looked on with suspicion, by both the head and the rest of the staff. The head thinks you're potentially a trouble-maker and maybe after his job and the staff think you're a toady. I hate it and it's this, more than anything else, which is making me look very hard for another job. I can't work if I don't believe I'm doing a good job and unless I get some feeling that others are satisfied too.
>
> (Lecturer, English)

The response of this staff member to overcoming her problems is to find another job and, at one level, this is a reasonable enough response, but it is not the one emphasized by Senge. His response is that no matter how brutish and nasty a situation may be, there is always something that can be done to make it better. This is a sentiment at the heart of the discipline of personal mastery but a sentiment rarely displayed during the interviews conducted with the academic staff (see Chapter 2). The following comment is particularly salient:

> There is an irony somewhere here that I can scrutinize and judge and comment on the political acts of kings and presidents and princes since the dawn of history and yet I find myself trapped by a bunch of amateur politicians in this university. I feel helpless to make an impact and change things for the better either for myself or my students. For the first time in my life, I feel a victim.
>
> (Senior lecturer, politics)

Senge emphasizes how vital it is not to feel a victim. Personal mastery is the ability to take account of the environment and work out what you as an individual can do to make things better – for yourself and for others.

Personal mastery has to be directed towards something, and that something is characterized by a vision – a personal vision. Personal visions might be thought to be a bit like dreams or wish lists, but we are told that this is not the case. Senge and others (Fritz 1989) emphasize that the development of a personal vision is not a trivial undertaking. According to Robert Fritz, upon whose work Senge draws considerably, developing a personal vision involves interrogating the often complex and competing demands in our life to establish what means most and what lies behind this. For instance, we might assume we want promotion, but when we ask ourselves why, we realize that what we really want is rather the respect of colleagues and to have greater influence. It might be that, upon reflection, we find that achieving respect and influence is more important than achieving promotion, and this is likely to be important to know when developing ourselves and directing our actions. According to Fritz, it is common to latch on to the means mistaking them for the deeper ends to which we truly aspire.

Personal visions must always be articulated and questioned and rearticulated with reference to our personal aspirations and capacities within the larger environment. Personal circumstances change and therefore so will personal visions. A major emphasis of Senge is the combining of personal, domestic and workplace visions. He insists that personal visions must go beyond the workplace and career. They must include, the whole life, domestic, social and leisure as well as work. If the total vision is not included, then one part of the vision can only thrive at the expense of another. The personal vision has to include all ambitions and hopes and they must be planned in concert with each other, not at the cost of one another. Employees have to be honest about stating their very personal ambitions and employers have to recognize the advantages in encouraging such statements.

Senge's argument is that we have grown to accept that personal life and interests are not the concern of employers but this is questionable. Perhaps some employers only want an honest day's work but in the learning organization the boundaries between work and private time must become increasingly blurred because problems and issues have to be addressed when they emerge, not when the workplan permits. Equally, children have illnesses and families have crises and they have to be attended to when they happen. There are twenty-four hours in a day and a learning organization and their staff have to use them flexibly.

Universities are organizations where this blurring of the boundaries has been long accepted. Academic staff work at home a good deal and have rarely started work or finished work on the dot of any hour. They work to the demands of the job rather than to the hours of any contract. As organizations, universities have often been amongst the most welcoming of family friendly policies and the most accepting of flexible ways of working. It is, therefore, disturbing to hear comments from the academic staff surveyed in Chapter 2 concerning the moves within their own universities towards tighter control of work practice and less tolerance of flexible ways of working:

> I now have to have the head of department's written permission if I want to work at home for any time outside the normal nine to five hours. I have also been told that I'm not to bring in my children when they are sick, nor allow them to come to me on their way home from school. How am I, as a single working mother, to organise my life? I used to believe that academic work was quite compatible to my personal and domestic needs . . . this appears to be the case no longer.
>
> (Lecturer, nursing)

Senge emphasizes that employees with troubled home lives, with ailing family relationships and breaking homes do not make for good employees and observes:

> The conflict between work and home is not just a conflict over time, but over values. All the habits that an executive learns in an authoritarian organization are exactly the habits . . . that make them unsuccessful parents. How can an executive build up a child's self-esteem at home when he or she is accustomed to tearing down other people's self-esteem at the office? The values and habits learned by practicing the five disciplines of a learning organization serve to nurture the family as well as the business. It's a virtuous circle: not only is being a good parent and partner a training ground for being a learningful manager, but being a learningful manager is also good preparation for parenting. The conflict between work and home diminishes dramatically when the organization fosters values in alignment with people's own core values that have equal meaning at work and at home.
>
> (Senge 1992: 312)

The first step in personal mastery is being clear and open about personal visions – those concerning our private as well as our professional life. Personal visions need continual clarification in the light of changing external circumstances and our developing personal capacity.

The second step involves not allowing yourself to be a victim but knowing that the world operates with little attention to our personal desires. People and things are not out to get us – on the whole, they are merely indifferent to us.

The third step involves finding ways to work towards our vision and being confident we are able to make a difference – even in the face of a seemingly hostile environment.

Mental models

Senge's mental models are the assumptions which underpin our knowing and doing. They are the premises on which we base our understanding of different aspects of the world and the way it works. In academic study, we might call them paradigms. It is the way that knowing is structured and it is against this structure that all evidence is judged. It is extraordinarily difficult to change because, once established, it becomes the mechanism through which all information is scrutinized and by which information which does not fit is rejected. In our academic life, we make our theoretical base explicit in an attempt to make development and change possible but in our everyday life we do not. Indeed, largely, we are not aware of the prejudices and assumptions which form the base of our everyday actions.

Senge suggests that workplaces are very often in conflict because of variation in mental models. One group works to one model of how things should be, whilst another group works to another model – and conflict prevails. The data in the survey of academic staff (reported in Chapter 2) suggest that academic work has its share of conflict in this respect. Here are two examples. First, the data suggest that those in leadership positions believe that to consult with staff will take a lot of time and they do not have a lot of time, so they avoid it. Staff, on the other hand, believe that decisions cannot be worthwhile ones unless they are consulted so they become angry when consultation does not take place. Secondly, amongst a good many staff in the survey, there was an assumption that less time and more students had to mean a lowering of standards. The following comment is typical:

> We can't possibly teach this many students and maintain the quality of results. The numbers are too high, the existing standard of entry is too low. The result has to be a lowering of standards. I've worked hard not to allow this to happen for a long time – but the circumstances now are just out of control.
>
> (Senior lecturer, chemistry)

But such an assumption is not universal, for instance:

> There's great pressure on all of us to do more . . . I don't think I've got the answer but I have found that by doubling on tute [tutorial] sizes, but providing tighter feedback mechanisms we can free up a lot of time. In effect instead of teaching for twelve weeks of the semester staff are only teaching core stuff for six. Now this allows time for two things. First, coping with major problems that some students will have run into, sort of remedial stuff and also time for research. It's certainly worked well enough for us to continue the experiment for another year. The students

> have done better, on the whole and we've freed up staff from core teaching and got a more focused and productive research program.
> (Associate professor, electrical engineering)

Unearthing and recognizing our own mental models, and those of our colleagues, is vital in overcoming conflict and working towards shared ends.

Senge suggests that the way forward is through self-scrutiny and reflection and a conscious shift from advocacy to inquiry. Typically, as professionals, we are more inclined to sell something and act as advocate than we are to enquire about something and test our assumptions and genuinely seek out evidence to help us to do this. Advocacy is important because it is important to make our position explicit. But before we practise advocacy, we must practise inquiry and scrutinize the values and assumptions at the core of our advocated positions.

Senge's development of the idea of mental models was based a good deal on the work of Chris Argyris and Donald Schön (1978) who explored the ways in which people in organizations construct what Argyris called 'defensive routines' which hide people's vulnerability and stop both discussion and debate. Argyris and Schön's argument was that people espouse one set of values in discussion (those which they believe to be morally sound) but that they act on another set of values (those which ensure they protect their own vulnerability). Twenty years or more before the literature on learning organizations was developed, Argyris and Schön hypothesized that we have a set of theories for our actions – a set of rules – designed to guide our individual behaviour and this is what we espouse and how we claim to act. These theories are those we believe to be moral and right and those we would choose to act upon if other things did not get in the way. In reality, other things *do* get in the way, particularly when we work in organizations. For when we work in organizations, we feel under pressure and under scrutiny and so we often work defensively. Argyris and Schön undertook literally hundreds of empirical studies and, subsequently, identified the way people typically do act in organizations – the theory in use. They identified four fundamental needs which guide the way they act. The need to:

- remain in control;
- maximize winning and minimize losing;
- suppress negative feelings; and
- be as 'rational' as possible – that is to define objectives and to evaluate behaviours in terms of whether or not objectives are achieved.

The purpose is to avoid embarrassment or threat, feeling vulnerable or incompetent. The result of this is that people, particularly professional people, go into a situation much more concerned about maintaining their face and avoiding unpleasant exchanges than about listening to their colleagues and learning. But they never see this because they assume they act according to espoused theory and they never get down to examining their actual theory in action. Many of the investigations were conducted in education, in government and in the church as well as in business organizations. The same mode of working was found in different types of organizations.

Argyris and Schön developed two models of working in organizations (Schön 1983; Argyris 1985). Model 1 exemplifies the type of behaviours explained above. In this model, staff aim to be as self-contained as possible. They keep negative feelings to themselves and they discourage others from speaking their minds on matters which worry them. In this way, they try to protect themselves and to deflect contention. Argyris and Schön emphasize that, primarily, individuals are working to defend themselves from change. These individuals believe that, on the whole, the way they work and what they produce is fine the way it is and, if change has to happen, then others can do it.

Model 2 patterns of working try to open up the system for debate and questioning. They encourage individuals and groups to reflect on the process of working with others, as well as the aims and visions behind their work. Above all, they encourage openness and honesty. No doubt we all believe that Model 2 patterns are worthy, they would likely be our espoused theories, but when faced with a situation in which we feel vulnerable (which is often in our working lives), we tend to defend ourselves and revert to Model 1-type actions.

Argyris and Schön emphasize the extreme challenge facing those who wish to adopt Model 2 ways of working. It is not enough to want it to happen; there have to be robust support systems in place to encourage it to happen. Paradoxically, when we start feeling vulnerable, we stop being open. There is a deeper issue here as well. Even when we try to be open and to strive to overcome our feelings of vulnerability, we are likely to misread situations and the actions both of ourselves and others and end up moving back into defensive mode. Argyris and Schön explain that in reading a situation we are likely to make leaps of abstraction which cause bias in our interpretation. By way of example, a member of academic staff might believe that he is never consulted on curriculum matters, so when his head of department calls a meeting to discuss new curriculum, he does not attend because he does not believe that he will be listened to. He interprets the meeting as a sham. If he goes he will just waste his time. So, the head complains to the dean that staff do not respond to his calls for input and the staff member continues to believe that he is never consulted.

Argyris and Schön have developed a technique for helping staff to unearth the assumptions which underpin their action. It is a simple and powerful technique which involves recalling a specific exchange with a colleague or group of colleagues where there was conflict or where communication did not appear to be effective. The technique involves dividing a report sheet into two columns. On the right-hand side, the conversation between the parties, that is what was actually said, is recorded. On the left-hand side, participants record their thoughts as the conversation progressed; the thoughts that preceded their own comments and the thoughts (as opposed to the words) which followed the comments of their colleague(s). This process helps people become aware of, and reflect on, their own, often previously unarticulated, responses to a given situation.

Let us practice this technique with a hypothetical exchange between the lecturer and head of department given above as an example. The lecturer was convinced that he was never consulted but he was asked by his head of department to attend a meeting on developing a new curriculum. We adopt the role of the lecturer and the 'what I'm thinking' column is completed from the lecturer's point of view.

What is said	*What I'm thinking*
Head of department: Did you get notice of the curriculum meeting? Not many people turned up. It would have been useful to have had the full teaching team there. I'd like to hear everyone's point of view about where we go from here with this course.	
Me (lecturer): I'm sorry it's just such a busy time of the year.	*Me (lecturer):* My workload is intolerable and he expects me to turn up to meetings which are just a waste of time because nothing I say will make any difference.
Head of department: We're having another meeting next week, Friday at lunch-time. I really would like you to come along. I'm making a special request because I know you have some comments to make about the way we are currently managing things and about how we might change next year.	
Me (lecturer): I'll try, but I'm doing a series of tutes at the moment with a few students who have hit problems because of the cut-back in contact time. I've arranged a session for Friday but I'll try to change it.	*Me (lecturer):* I don't believe it. I'm trying to save us from dreadful failure rates and all he's interested in is having a sham consultation. He knows what I feel about this course, the way it's run now and he's not going to change a thing.
Head of department: It would be good if you could do that. I look forward to seeing you.	

This exercise always brings hidden assumptions to the surface and shows how they can influence behaviour. In the case above, the lecturer (the 'I' role) assumes that there is no intention on the part of the head to genuinely seek consultation and take advice. The lecturer assumes that the exercise is a sham. He also assumes that the reason the students are not doing well is because of changes in the course. Neither of these two assumptions is made explicit in the conversation with the head, neither is there any attempt to check these assumptions in any way.

Let us now move the scenario on to the meeting itself and swap roles. The 'I' figure is now the head of department.

What is said	*What I'm thinking*
Me (head of department): We have had to make changes to the course because of funding cuts. The bottom line is, there isn't the money for tutorials. We've cut contact time, mainly tutorials and I know that's been hard for you and the students but I want to consider next year and listen to any comments you might have about how things have gone and how we might handle it next year.	*Me (head of department):* This is going to be a difficult meeting. They don't want to be here. They don't want to face the problems the course is confronting. They're not prepared to seriously address the issues. All they want to do is complain about any initiatives I try to take.
Lecturer: The students are finding it hard. We need to reinstate the tutes [tutorials]. The only reason the results are not worse is because the teaching staff are putting more in – in feedback and non-timetabled tutes. We can't get by without more contact time as far as I can see.	*Me (head of department):* Don't they listen? I've said the bottom line is that there's no more funding. They can't begin to think laterally. It's left up to me to come up with the ideas and then they reject them.
Lecturer: That's right, we can't offer a quality course without more contact time. Our standards will drop.	*Me (head of department):* I knew this meeting was a waste of time. They're just not prepared to change.

The assumptions on the part of the head is that the staff are not willing or able to think outside of the traditional model of university teaching. He stops listening to what they say as soon as they do not attend to his comment that the financial imperative makes more staffing impossible. He despairs that the staff do not think laterally, but he does not help or encourage them to do so.

Undertaking exercises, such as the one above, is one way of unearthing hidden assumptions and questioning them, but the principle to focus upon is that staff, at all levels, need to constantly question their assumptions and a good deal of encouragement and support is essential if this is to happen.

Let us briefly summarize what has been stated so far concerning mental models. Mental models are the prejudices and assumptions which inform our everyday thinking and doing. They are often the things which get in the way of us working positively together and learning from experiences. Our commitment to existing mental models means that we are often not tuned to learning, but to defensiveness and to appearing rational in advocating our existing position. Although as academic staff, like all other professionals, we can eloquently defend our actions with high-sounding moral theories, more often than not we work in order to remain in control, maximize winning and minimize losing, and suppress negative feelings. To be more open and honest, we have to become vulnerable; we have to open up to the possibilities of losing control, of not winning – and doing this during a time of change is challenging and courageous. Academic staff need the concerted support and help of their universities if this is to happen.

Shared vision

We work enthusiastically towards a vision when the vision is our own. But, typically, organizations see it as their responsibility to provide staff with visions to follow. Senior leaders take time out to create their own vision and they then pass it down the hierarchy. At one level, they know that it will not enthuse and galvanize staff into spirited action, but they assume that with sufficient 'stick and carrot' enough staff will be moved towards compliance. Senge suggests this approach needs rethinking because compliance, in itself, is not enough. Organizations need commitment *not* compliance. Consequently, Senge argues for the idea of 'shared vision'.

Shared vision is built on the personal visions of individual staff and has to be rooted in the concerns and commitment of personal visions because caring is a personal phenomenon. We can, and do, care for things beyond the personal but that caring can only spring from personal concern based on personal values. The difference between commitment which springs from personal vision, and compliance which springs from buying into other people's visions, can be seen very clearly in our universities. As an example, many of the teaching staff of our universities care about their students. This is clear from the interviews collected in the survey of academic staff (see Chapter 2). Staff will often work long and hard to ensure that students achieve their potential and students know that they can count on these teaching staff. Universities, on the other hand, are less convinced they can count on staff because the demands made appear to staff to be things they simply do not care about – for instance, accountability systems or attracting global markets.

Of course, there are links between those things the university expects staff to do and those staff really do care about, between systems of accountability and the teaching of students, for instance, and shared visions are developed by collaboratively exploring those links. But this is often not the way organizational visions, including those of universities, develop. What often happens is that organizations create visions and mission and then work to get staff to comply. Those in leadership positions spend a good deal of time wondering how they can get those in non-leadership positions to buy into the handed-down organizational vision.

Senge (1992: 218) estimates that few subjects are closer to the heart of contemporary organizations than commitment because leaders know that organizations with high staff commitment work effectively but, in aiming for commitment, they often use the tools of compliance and the consequence is that 90 per cent of the time staff are not personally committed; they are only compliant. We can draw parallels with teachers, described in Chapter 3, who aimed for student learning but who, in using the tools of telling, achieved no more than surface responses from their students. To engage the commitment of staff is not dissimilar to engaging the commitment of students; there has to be explanation, debate, reflection and a willingness to try to see where others are coming from.

Senge hypothesizes that there are two types of learning in organizations: there is generative learning and adaptive learning. Generative learning is the sort of learning which builds on itself, which generates and refines questions and reflects on practice and knowledge, and which is undertaken out of genuine commitment and curiosity. Adaptive learning is the sort of learning people do when they have to. They have to learn to do things to comply with required conditions or attend to imposed tasks. Senge suggests that imposed visions encourage adaptive learning while shared visions excite generative learning. Once again, there is a clear parallel between deep and surface approaches to learning and the deep and surface outcomes discussed in Chapter 3.

The reason shared visions are so difficult to generate is that the view of many staff at the chalkface is so different to the view of others further up the hierarchy. Staff filling different roles in the organization have different horizons and therefore focus on different concerns. The example given in the previous section on mental models is useful. The lecturer and head of department were in conflict over reduced contact time and a lack of consultation. The day-to-day life of the lecturer focused on helping students to learn. He was keenly aware of the problems at this level. When asked to contribute to discussion on the course, this is naturally where he first focused. The head of department, however, had a different day-to-day reality which focused more on budgets and student numbers and attending to the demands of his boss, the dean. If the head consulted with staff, he wanted to hear how he could deal with the problem at his level, that is, how to teach students with fewer resources at his department's disposal. The focus of the lecturer, in contrast, is primarily upon the students. He maintains that an increase in student numbers will see a deterioration in teaching quality unless more resources are available.

When Senge talks of developing personal vision, he talks of being keenly aware of both the local environment and the wider environment. Similar advice is possibly even more salient at the level of shared vision. We have to know where our colleagues are in their thinking and we have to know where the larger environment is in its thinking and trends. Once again, we might draw a parallel with student learning. In Chapter 3, we emphasized that good teaching involved starting from where the student was in his or her understanding. Similarly, with developing a shared vision, it is necessary for staff at all levels to take into account where colleagues are likely to be coming from in their response to a situation.

It might have been thought that these differences of focus at different levels of the hierarchy were a major constraint in developing a shared vision but this is not necessarily the case. Richard T. Pascale (1990), another writer and researcher who has inspired much of Senge's work, argues that this tension is essential. Pascale points out the necessity for the creative use of conflict in organizations. He suggests that successful ways forward happen when there is first pressure and, ultimately, consensus from both above and from below. He maintains that an organization has to develop systems which promote the constructive use of questioning of all practice. The things the university sees as important for its current survival have to be presented and debated with staff, rather than imposed on them. Staff need opportunities to see how their university's concerns relate to their own concerns. Senior staff also need the insights of staff working at the chalkface.

In the author's own university, the vision behind attracting more international students has moved from one where economics and winning more fees dominated to one where curricula and learning experiences now dominate. This has happened because a few committed and imaginative staff members shared and extended their visions concerning what can be gained through exploring the relevant, varied background experiences of international students. In business, for instance, the notion of taxation or audit is taught as having a core meaning and then a fuller meaning is developed by considering the diverse ways in which these key concepts are interpreted by the different nations of the students in the class. The meaning is explored by considering variation within different contexts. Once internationalization meant problems with students who were unable to speak English and who were used to doing things differently. Now it means an opportunity to learn from diverse experiences. In this respect, at least, there is a shared vision.

Senge would argue that what happened, in the above example, was that a creative tension emerged. Individuals at all levels of the organization eventually shared a vision of where the organization might go but, initially, there was a good deal of disagreement. It is not that the views of everyone were considered equally; the university was not going to move against trends in the wider environment and cut back on accepting overseas students. However, the university was eventually willing to attend to the ideas of staff concerning how to reconceptualize the issue of teaching overseas students. In the end, a positive way forward emerged which caught the imagination of many people within the university and beyond. The idea was subsequently picked up by a number of other universities (Patrick 1996).

Coping with change in organizations

The problem in universities at the moment, of course, is that energy and commitment are, typically, not high. The feedback from staff presented in Chapter 2 suggests that in many academic environments, any request for staff to assist in developing a new vision will likely engender suspicion rather than excitement. The literature on coping with change in organizations is relevant here and we will digress slightly from the central theme of building a shared vision in order to attend to the issues this literature raises. Focus will mostly be on the work of William Bridges (1991). Bridges works on a simple three-stage model. The first stage involves letting go of existing practices (*attending to endings*). The second stage involves seeking out, and giving, support during the transition time, that is, the period of waiting before the new situation has emerged (*managing the transition zone*). The third stage involves making beginnings as positive as possible (*launching a new beginning*). Each of these stages is discussed below.

Attending to endings

Bridges is a psychologist who has done substantial work on loss and grieving. He emphasizes that letting go of things once cherished will involve feelings of loss and resentment at best – possibly even anger and despair. What is often seen as overreaction – emotional outbreaks, illogical claims and threatening behaviour – is to be expected. The more staff care about their work, and university staff characteristically care a good deal, the more such behaviour should be anticipated and acknowledged as a reasonable grieving process rather than as an unreasonable overreaction. When something valued is lost, it is simply not possible to pick up the next thing and straight away carry on. Such behaviour would be thought callous if the loss were a personal one, but when the loss is a professional one, it is often expected that staff will just carry on with whatever life or work they have left. We know a good deal about the deleterious effect of loss of work. We know it causes major emotional trauma and serious questioning of self-worth; we should not expect ourselves and others just to let go and get on.

Bridges suggests two other strategies for coping with the loss (other than accepting and expecting emotional behaviour). The first involves acknowledging the quality of the thing which is lost. When something valued is to be replaced, its worth appears especially great and it is not helpful to suggest that it was outdated or ill-conceived. All practices and groupings have a time of value and a time when changes must be made. This is the time to celebrate the value of what is lost whilst acknowledging the need to move on. People need to have reaffirmed that the things to which they have committed a number of their working years were indeed worthwhile, that there have been a number of excellent outcomes and that perhaps the underpinning principles and values can be built on. For instance, no-one denies that teaching students in small groups of three or four is not an excellent way to organize learning or that this way of teaching is potentially highly beneficial for both students and staff. The fact it can no longer be practised in many, if not most universities, does not mean its intrinsic qualities are diminished.

The second strategy is to share and access information about what is happening in the larger environment. Not just why did it happen here to us, but where else in the system is this happening and how are others responding? We need to identify the meta-trends which are affecting all similar organizations. We need to do this so that we are able to learn from others but also so that blaming and bitterness are minimized at the local level. In the case study in Chapter 9, we will see how the staff from two very different departments, one a department of tourism and leisure, the other of sociology, respond to a merger. The initial response is to blame local colleagues. It takes a lot of work on the part of a few to help all staff see that the loss of their department is not the simple result of an individual's ambition or negligence. The reasons are complex but they are not just local; demands in the larger system for efficiencies of scale, for moves towards more vocational courses will contribute a good deal more towards the need for change than any local factors and no-one can be blamed for these.

Senge writes of the need to look at the whole system and attend to mega- as well as meta-trends for an understanding of why things are as they are as well as how they might change. This is a critical lesson to be learned in this early stage of attending to the loss.

Managing the transition zone

The literature on change suggests that beginnings do not actually follow on from endings; there is a transition period and for many people this is the most difficult time. This is the time when frustration and tension are high and when people often become polarized between those who want to rush ahead and those who want to hold back and return to the old ways. It is also a time when those in the organization who are demanding the changes are likely to get impatient for things to start happening. If we are in such positions of authority ourselves, we need to be aware that the most successful changes are by no means those that happen quickest. This point is picked up a little later on in this section.

It was stressed earlier that shared visions develop out of personal visions. This transition time is an excellent period in which to seriously reassess our personal visions. What do these changes mean for our own future? Some doors are closing but others are also opening and what might this mean for our own development as well as for that of the team?

Pascale (1990) emphasizes that one of the major benefits of change is that we are forced into a situation whereby we have to think creatively about future options and responses. We tend not to think too creatively when systems or plans are running smoothly. It is hard to change things, to do something new or different without a push. But once circumstances give us that push then thinking creatively and laterally about how to use the situation becomes the reasonable and shrewd rather than speculative thing to do. Bridges (1991) suggests that it is useful at these times to have workshops and discussions which deliberately encourage creative and lateral thinking about options. It helps generate a sense of excitement about further possibilities and helps minimize the tendency to look back towards what is lost.

It was emphasized earlier that the transition zone is a time when some in a group will be able to rush forward and think creatively about the future but others will need to take longer to lament the loss. At such times, long-term planning for the group is difficult. Bridges suggests that short-term planning, however, is potentially most beneficial. It is useful because it keeps the group together and it keeps individuals involved. Such planning and goals might include conducting a survey of other groups similarly affected. It might be: a review of market trends; an evaluation of aspects of present practice; an assessment of what activities are valuable and productive and might be continued and what is not working. At another level, it might even be the planning of a formal event to mark the loss of a particular practice or a group.

It is appropriate, once again, to mention the case study in Chapter 9. Many members of staff from the two merging departments of this case study felt a reluctance to let go of their old departments and to move on. It was, consequently, agreed to organize a series of events to celebrate the achievements of both departments over the previous years. The events enabled staff to work positively together. It allowed them to acknowledge that things were changing and helped them to move towards thinking how the strengths of the two merging teams might complement each other in the future.

The important thing is that during this transition time, there is a need to be active and engaged with issues central to the change. In times of change, patterns of sickness and absenteeism are a well-documented phenomena. We should not get too concerned if they happen occasionally, but once this becomes the only way of responding, it will take a long time to recover self-confidence and achieve positive outcomes. If we can find relevant short-term goals to help us through this difficult time, we will ultimately feel the benefit.

Launching a new beginning

The third – and final – stage of the model of change involves making a new beginning. New beginnings will likely be boldly launched and formally planned at the institutional level, but at the local level staff are more likely to have had a few planning meetings and then be expected to get on with it. Bridges stresses that staff need to ask, and to be supported in answering, the following four questions:

- What is the new shared vision or picture – what will it look like?
- What is the new purpose – what is it for?
- What is the plan – how will we get there?
- What part will each individual play?

When two departments merge, for instance, there are institutional consequences and objectives which will have to be sorted out and attended to student records, budget, buildings, reporting, advertising – all this will usually happen, and it is assumed that the new beginning is on its way. But there are many changes which have to happen for staff within the departments which are likely to be overlooked. Even when staff have agreed upon, and worked collaboratively towards, the new beginning it is important to ensure that they embark on the change with their personal picture of, and purpose for, the new combined department well established. They have to be sure how things will get done and they have to have an idea of where they, as individuals, will fit in and how they will contribute. Without people at the base level having a picture, a purpose, a plan and a part, new beginnings – no matter how well planned at an institutional level – will likely not be successful.

Shared vision revisited

We now return to the discussion of shared vision which is the third of Senge's disciplines. We digressed in order to acknowledge that it is hard to win the commitment of academic staff at a time when so many staff are demoralized. Senge insists that it is commitment – not compliance – which is necessary for the development of a committed vision and we looked at the work of Bridges to see how such a commitment may be developed in a positive fashion.

We now conclude this section by summarizing the key issues necessary for developing the discipline of shared vision:

- First, shared vision begins with personal vision. An organization lacking in personal vision will not develop vigorous, and enabling, shared visions.
- Secondly, shared visions develop in a climate of creative tension. Creative tensions emerge when staff articulate the issues which mean most to them, but also toil to see the salience of issues raised by those in different positions who attend to different pressures.
- Thirdly, shared visions, once forged, stimulate commitment and enthusiasm and this takes individuals and organizations infinitely further than does compliance.
- Fourthly, it is hard to develop commitment to a new way when one is mourning the loss of once-valued work practices. Time, tolerance and understanding are needed to help all of us through this loss and towards new aspirations.

Team learning

A good deal of myth and illusion surrounds the idea of teams. They are the basis for most of the work which goes on in organizations yet, so often, they are the bastions of conflict and aggravation where more time is spent in internal battles than in addressing any major external challenges. Senge tells us that:

> All too often teams in business tend to spend their time fighting for turf and avoiding anything that will make them look bad personally, and pretending that everyone is behind the team's collective strategy – maintaining the *appearance* of a cohesive team. To keep up the image, they seek to squelch disagreement; people with serious reservations avoid stating them publicly, and joint decisions are watered-down compromises.
>
> (Senge 1992: 24)

Senge (ibid.: 10) has described good team work as a process of aligning and developing the capacity of a team to work towards a common purpose and to create the results its members truly desire. He argues that successful teams generate knowledge and insights which address immediate problems but also provide an environment in which members learn how to address future problems. Senge (ibid.: 239) picks up on the work of David Bohm, the American quantum theorist, who has developed a theory of dialogue which models scientific work. Bohm suggests that meaning grows when the individual particles of knowledge or understanding which people produce fuse together to form a whole. This whole has a capacity and potential far greater than the sum of the parts.

Senge also argues that it is not just the expansion of knowledge which is significant; it is the learning which goes on during the process. Once group members have experienced this sort of team work and knowledge generation then they are in a good position to work in similar ways in other groups. Part of the problem (Schrage 1995) is that we often have no model of good team practice and, consequently, pay little attention to what better team work might entail. A good deal of our work as academic staff is done in teams – all of them quite different: teaching teams; research teams; academic committees. We, increasingly, encourage our students to undertake assignments and to study in teams, yet our own understanding of the purpose and the potential of team work is very undeveloped. A recent Australian study of teaching teams found that for a significant proportion of academic staff, the teaching team is no more than a loose linking of colleagues who taught specific subject content and who added their self-contained parcel of knowledge to the overall programme (Benjamin 1997). There was, normally, a coordinator who ensured that one sequence followed another, for instance, that rooms were booked and assessments given and marks handed in – but there was minimal collaboration amongst the staff themselves concerning new directions or synthesis. Of course, there are excellent teaching teams but, on the whole, the teaching team is not widely recognized for its ability to work in an exemplary way.

Team work is about working towards a common purpose and our teaching teams usually have the common purpose of contributing to a programme of study and helping students to learn. Our university committees, on the other hand, often appear extraordinarily divided on common purpose and appear remarkably close to Senge's descriptions of management teams in business who often spend their time 'fighting for turf, advocating their own views and blocking the views of others' (ibid.: 24). A reading of almost any academic novel (those of C.P. Snow, for instance) adds credence to the belief that the academic committees are more often a political device concerned with governance and power rather than an efficient team concerned with learning.

There is one type of team in academia, however, which collects accolades from writers on organizational learning and that is the research team (Fullan 1994; Schrage 1995). Research teams are created to complement the strengths and qualities of individual members. They come together by design and desire rather than by accident or necessity. They come together with a common purpose, that of addressing a major problem or issue. They work insightfully and critically, that is, they collect evidence and question that evidence. Members build on, and spark off, each other's insights and they take the 'collective knowing' way beyond that of the individual knowing. Senge (ibid.: 9) comments that a research team when coming together will likely have a collective capacity many times more than the sum capacity of the individual members. A management team, however, he cynically suggests, often has the capacity of little more than half the capacity of any single member of the team.

It is rare and refreshing for a part of academic culture to be held up as an example of good practice by the business world, but those of us who are familiar with research teams know that the above descriptions draw a good deal on best-case scenarios. There are considerable differences in the ways research teams work in different disciplines but, overall, there are some common negatives to balance the previous positives. Research teams are often hierarchical with chief investigators doing little data collection or basic analysis and yet making all the major decisions. Sometimes, there is competition and rivalry between members of the team and heated divisions are not that uncommon. What does unite the team, however, is a commitment to the initial issue or problem and this unity can usually overcome substantial problems and ensure that the team functions effectively, all be it, sometimes, painfully.

In summary, then, it has been argued that team learning goes way beyond the knowing or learning of any single member of the team. Team learning involves the developing of a collective pool of knowledge out of which new insights and awareness emerge. For Senge, team learning is vital because the complexity of the contemporary environment means that an individual's learning and knowing can never be enough to keep across developments and to generate responses. Unless teams can work together effectively and learn, then organizations will not develop the capacity to be responsive.

Systems thinking

Systems thinking, the fifth discipline, is the task of making sense of the parts. Senge draws the analogy of a storm:

> . . . a cloud masses, the sky darkens, leaves twist upward, and we know that it will rain. We also know that after the rain, the runoff will feed into ground water miles away, and the sky will grow clear by tomorrow. All of these events are distant in time and space, and yet they are all connected within the same pattern. Each has an influence on the rest, an influence that is usually hidden from view. You can only understand the system of a rainstorm by contemplating the whole, not any individual part of the pattern.
>
> (Senge 1992: 6)

Senge reminds us that human actions are also systems and, whether we intend it or not, they are bound by the 'invisible fabric' of interrelated actions. Because we are part of the pattern ourselves, it is hard to step back and see the whole pattern. We tend, instead, to focus on local parts of the pattern which obviously, and immediately, relate to us. Because of this, the deepest parts of the problem usually remain unaddressed; indeed, they may even become aggravated.

Senge argues that the ability and will to become involved in systems thinking is not, in itself, difficult; experiments with primary school children demonstrate that they can very quickly develop the ability to adopt systems thinking. The difficult thing is to see the complexity of the system in which we, as individuals, are involved. This requires thinking beyond simple linear explanations – for instance, that our colleagues or our leaders or our government or something else out there is the cause of the problem. We have to come to terms with the fact that there is no out there, that we are all part of the problem because we are all part of a single system.

This does not mean that there is nothing that can be done. Quite the contrary. It means that once we see the system as a whole, we can see the point in the system where the least effort will have the most effect. We can see where we, or our team, can make a difference. Senge begins his book with the quote: 'Give me a lever long enough . . . and single-handed I can move the world.' He does not suggest that we do it single-handedly. Rather, he suggests that we work as individuals with a personal vision in teams which have a shared vision to open ourselves and our colleagues and our organizations to the excitement and satisfaction of learning.

Conclusion

Senge's five disciplines combine to create a powerful meta-system which has the capacity both to move and influence the larger one. There are significant challenges in developing these disciplines, not least that we have to unlearn ways of working which we have practised all of our professional lives – the defensive routines described by Argyris and Schön (1978) for instance. But to work towards the development of these disciplines is clearly possible as well as desirable. It is possible because learning is a basic human drive which most healthy people – certainly professional people – choose to pursue. It is desirable because no-one wants to spend the remainder of their working lives engaged in tasks which breed anguish and leach satisfaction.

Senge argues that staff must develop these five disciplines – personal mastery; mental models; shared vision; team learning; and systems thinking – in order to assist their organizations to learn and to change in the current, constantly changing environment. On the surface, Senge's disciplines have much in common with the fundamental principles of collegiality (for instance, to work within an acknowledged paradigm with a considered but firm individual position, but equally to engage in debate with colleagues and be open to their insights; these are working codes long cherished by academic staff). However, to read Senge's argument in this way would be to see only the superficial similarities with collegiality and to miss the significant differences. The ways of working in the traditional university and the new learning organization may be similar but the ends are very different. In established academe, work has traditionally been directed towards preserving existing knowledge and cautiously edging forward with new knowledge and ways of working. In the new university, and in the learning organization, the aim is to be continually adaptive rather than cautiously so. The new university work, then, becomes radically different to the old, with staff using their well-established ability to think and to reason and to collaborate with the aim of serving change rather than constraining it.

5

Finding a Way Forward

> Confusion is a word we have invented for an order which is not yet understood.
>
> (Henry Miller)

Introduction

This chapter is an important one because it brings together the key issues raised in Chapter 2 concerning the way academic staff work together. It sets these concerns against the relevant literature on student learning and on organizational change which has been discussed in Chapters 3 and 4, and it flags ways forward which could make working in an academic environment more rewarding and more productive for staff within universities.

We begin with a table which summarizes much of what has been said in previous chapters. The columns in Table 5.1 emphasize key comments from university staff, from their leaders, from the student learning literature and from the learning organization literature. The rows indicate four areas of major concern. This table will be used to overview what has been said in previous chapters and to flag what is argued in the following chapters. Reading down the first column, it is easy to pick out the main issues. Put simply, academic staff in non-leadership positions have a perception that those in leadership positions provide them with little or misguided vision and direction. They believe there is little attempt to work either collaboratively or to involve them in decision-making. They recognise that accountability is now a fact of academic life, but they perceive this accountability to be wrapped in excessively bureaucratic processes which get in the way of the core university work – teaching and research. Furthermore, these accountability processes appear unrelated to the main reward systems of university life. Underpinning all of this is the conviction that the university does not care about its staff. The comments, sometimes to be found in policy documents, that people are the institution's most important resource,

Table 5.1 The concerns of academic staff and advice as expressed through the literature

Area of concern			
Academic staff in non-leadership roles say:	*Academic staff in leadership roles say:*	*Student learning literature says:*	*Learning organization literature says:*
'Senior university leaders have limited or flawed vision.'	'Staff will not change.'	'Learners need to see the salience of what they are being asked to learn and how they are being asked to change.'	'The needs and strengths of staff, as well as the force of external demands, require attention.'
'Decisions are made with little or no consultation or collaboration.'	'Academic staff find discussion more enchanting than decision-making.' 'Changes have to be pushed through. Discussion is non-productive.'	'Learners must engage with the learning task.' 'Learners need guidance as well as independence to learn.'	'Shared commitment, not imposition and mandate, brings about successful change.' 'Independence and self-reliance are essential for collaboration.'
'Excessive scrutiny and accountability gets in the way of real work.' 'Accountability is not linked to recognition and reward.'	'Accountability exists at all levels of university work. We are now all accountable.' 'Accountability has advantages – some staff need to be made more accountable.'	'Assessment must link to desired learning. Desired learning must be what is rewarded and recognized.' 'Assessment processes must support not get in the way of desired learning.'	'Develop organizational structures which support and reward the desired learning processes and outcomes.'
'People are not valued. Their past and present achievements are ignored.'	'Leaders also feel undervalued and undersupported.' 'Staff complain too much. Change agendas have to be attended to otherwise departments and/ or units will close, jobs will go.'	'Regular and supportive feedback is necessary for learning. Learning involves change.'	'Change can be painful but also liberating.' 'Support, including the opportunity for new learning and for personal development, is essential.'

are seen as rhetoric. Academic staff in non-leadership positions believe that the significant goals they have already achieved are inadequately appreciated. The focus is always on the future, and on more change, with minimal respect or gratitude for either the past or the present.

In the second column, we see how those staff with leadership responsibilities, at the level of head of course, head of department, or above perceive the situation differently. A major concern of these leaders is that academic staff are reluctant to change. There is frustration at the way academic staff debate and prevaricate and, in the end, change nothing. As a consequence, leaders often do not consult, but push necessary changes through by mandate or imposition. Concerning accountability, these leaders accept it as inevitable. It is a way of working with some irritations but also some advantages. In particular, it ensures that those who, in the past, have worked for their own ends rather than for the good of the department or university, can be challenged. Overall, leaders agree that morale may be low but it does not do any good to complain. The change agenda has to be attended to, otherwise units or departments or even whole universities might be closed and jobs will be lost.

Here are two different ways of seeing the same story; the story of changing work in universities. There is sufficient consistency within each of the groups to suggest that these two different clusters of perceptions represent the experience of a good many university staff. It is pointless to argue which of these two ways of seeing embody more or less objective truth. This is the way university work is experienced and perceived by representatives of the two groups and, as was argued in Chapter 3, the way it is perceived is important. It is important because the way something is perceived affects how people work.

The aim of this book is to find insights and guidance within the literature on student learning and organizational learning to help university people to work more effectively. The final two columns of the table suggest what these insights might be.

We will now develop the link between the concerns of staff and the insights and advice contained in the literature.

Vision and direction

In the interviews, staff complained that although existing ways of working were under attack, there was a lack of real vision for the future. New ideas emerged but these were neither exciting and visionary nor reasonable and feasible. Staff complained that it was hard to abandon long-cherished traditions when the vision of the future was uncertain or just plain silly:

> It's hard to follow unquestioningly when those who lead you are blind or blinkered.
>
> (Senior lecturer, psychology)

Other staff emphasized that the new directions did not begin to engage with the problems experienced by staff at the chalkface:

> It's easy to have a so-called good idea and send a memo to deans, but have they ever thought what it means in terms of changes in our work and lives?
>
> (Senior lecturer, business)

We discerned from the student learning literature how learners must see the salience of what they are being asked to do and to learn. If the students are helped to see that a goal is appropriate and, if they are offered support and guidance to achieve that goal, then they will more likely become committed. If, on the other hand, they feel that what they are being asked to do is inappropriate or impossible, there will likely be little commitment and little of worth will result.

Academic staff, in our higher education systems, are responding in a similar way to how students would respond in similar learning circumstances. The staff are reluctant to change because they cannot see the reason or the purpose for change and there appear to be limited opportunities and processes for them to be helped to see this purpose and to share their concerns and views with senior staff.

The learning organization literature tells us that the mismatch of views between leaders and staff which has been noted is not only to be expected, it is essential if there is to be learning and growth in the organization. The development of visions and missions necessarily start from a position of discord because staff and leaders inhabit different worlds but they must come together if the organization is to move forward efficiently. The exercise of collaboration required in this coming together involves very senior staff and very traditional academic staff to change: to rethink their position a little and to attend to different points of view. This is an infinitely more challenging task than getting students, who are less set in their thoughts and ways, to change but it must happen if a shared position is to emerge and purposeful change is to result. The wisdom and goodwill of academic staff in non-leadership positions is essential if productive change is to happen in our universities. Staff can be bullied into compliance and do the minimum, similar to those students who adopt surface approaches. But, as was seen in Chapter 3, useful, heuristic outcomes do not result from surface approaches.

Consultation in decision-making

More than anything else, academic staff in the survey complained about not being consulted and about discussion around important issues being stopped or ignored. At one level, it was argued that such a way of working was antipathetic to traditional collegiate values and that such actions were disempowering and demoralizing. But, at another level, it was argued that the consequence of lack of consultation were bad decisions. As one respondent commented:

> The trouble with senior leaders taking decisions is that they are uninformed as to the consequences. In cutting this research centre, we cut connections with industry and considerable potential for overseas collaboration and probably funding. That can't be in anyone's interest.

Those in leadership positions, however, emphasized that if staff were left to debate and discuss issues, nothing would happen and, in a contemporary university, decisions have to be made quickly.

There is a compelling parallel between the comments of fraught teachers as they push their way through a crowded curriculum and what university leaders say here. Both are concerned with the pressure of the work to be done and both feel that the only way to get it done is to take the action and responsibility themselves. So, teachers tell students what they have to learn because it is quicker and easier than getting the students to engage with the ideas and arrive at their own understanding. And university leaders tell academic staff what decisions have been made and what must be done because in the short term it is quicker and easier than having staff engage in debate and arrive at a workable way forward. Of course, not all academic work involves collaborative decision-making. Day-to-day work entails a good deal which is routine and rule-following, just as student learning involves recalling factual material and following procedures. But such rule-following has to be seen as a means to a salient end and staff, like students, need to engage in discussion around that salient end, otherwise, as was suggested earlier, the result will likely be superficial and meaningful outcomes will not result.

It has been mentioned above that getting academic staff to change their way of seeing is a challenging task. We are, on the whole, people with robust individual perspectives and opinions. We do not take change lightly. It is, therefore, almost anti-intuitive to learn from the learning organization literature that this ability to hold opinion robustly is indeed a virtue rather than a failing in group work and collaboration. The reason is that the aim of collaboration is not compliance but creativity. The group must both learn from each other and spark off each other to reach new insights and positions. The final position reached by the group is all the more durable because of the varied input.

Accountability

In the course of the interviews, the staff told us that accountability may be necessary, but the increased bureaucracy which often accompanied it was certainly not. Staff saw documentation getting in the way of the main university business – that of teaching and research. As one staff member put it:

> We are focusing on the documentation and forgetting the real thing. We're satisfying the university with the outward appearance, but nobody gives a damn about the real thing any more.

There was also concern that the aspects of university life which were open to increasing scrutiny – teaching in particular – were not the things that counted in terms of formal rewards:

> I endlessly fill in forms and create columns on spreadsheets to show how everything I am doing is accountable and the best . . . but I know it's a sham . . . and so does the university . . . because when it comes to the real rewards . . . the promotions, this counts for nothing. It's how many publications I've got that scores.

Those in leadership positions also made comment about demands for accountability. One head of department suggested that showing the university and the larger community that his department was accountable was the biggest single aspect of his job. He believed that it took around 75 per cent of his time.

There were, however, those in leadership positions who saw virtue in increased scrutiny; for instance, it helped keep in check members of staff who worked for their own advancement rather than for the good of the department or the institution:

> There are those who employ tutors with research funding and further enhance their own research reputations through doing minimal teaching. This sort of thing has to be stopped. We now have things documented to ensure this doesn't happen.

The lack of ties between the desired changes in university work, accountability mechanisms and the reward systems, is a repeated theme in staff comment. Currently, accountability mechanisms often appear to conflict with, rather than support, both the main business of the university and the traditional reward systems of the university. The most obvious rewards of the undergraduate course are university grades. This is what staff know students attend to and what they must regard when devising student learning experiences. The most obvious rewards of the academic system are promotion and reputation and, currently, these often appear to have little to do with formal accountability structures. If we attend to the student learning literature then universities will think hard about the links between reward and accountability.

In drawing the parallel with student assessment, we must remember that students get assessed very frequently – and grades are consequently a workable currency. Academic staff, on the other hand, receive formal promotion rarely and, consequently, the currency of promotion is less workable. In some universities, reward might be linked to personal or group performance plans but even this will happen no more than once a year. A more common currency is required and it is suggested there is one in use and that is professional reputation. Staff work, perhaps above all else, to enhance their reputation. The reputation of a staff member can be significantly enhanced or reduced through public acknowledegment, through the provision of additional responsibilities and freedoms or the loss of those responsibilities and freedoms. These sorts of non-structural rewards are likely to be significant in working out the balance between accountability and reward.

Recognition and support

The recent achievements of universities and those who work within them are legion. They include monumental changes in who is taught and what is taught and how it is taught. Academic staff often believe they have done well to accomplish what they have, yet they also feel that these achievements are unrecognized by their masters and by the system. The focus is not on what has been achieved, but what is still to be done. There is little attention to past success but much focus on the future and fresh challenges and changes.

Those in leadership positions also express feelings of being undervalued and ever-driven, but those in senior leadership positions are more ready, or able, to justify the need for constant change and limited consolidation. They are more in control of events and they can see the big picture more easily. They argue, for instance, that without still more change, student numbers will drop, funds will run out, departments or units may have to down-size or amalgamate or close and jobs – even more jobs – will be lost, so the pressure has to be kept up. They believe this to be true and, from their vantage point, are regularly confronted with evidence of this. They cannot understand why academic staff at their different position in the hierarchy cannot also see this.

Staff who are expected to pick up on wave after wave of change and new initiatives are less able to see the virtue or necessity in such a pattern of working. Even those who were once willing become disillusioned, when repeated efforts to do their best in difficult circumstances go unrewarded, and the emphasis is ever on new and more, rather than on the excellence already achieved.

The student learning literature emphasizes that learning is change, that is, change in ways of seeing and understanding. In order to foster change, you need to first of all accept and value the student's point of view but then you need to work in order to show the student that there exists a different, and probably more appropriate, way of thinking and perceiving. This involves close scrutiny of the work students do and the offering of constructive and critical comment on that work. It involves acknowledging success, but ever encouraging movement towards still greater accomplishments and changes.

The learning organization literature emphasizes the significant trauma which can be caused by changes in working life and the support and guidance which is needed to help staff through these times. It also emphasizes the potential excitement and creativity which can abound. Support has to come through opportunities for new learning and personal development and this support has to involve helping staff to let go of the practice of the past as well as to prepare for the future.

Emerging tensions

What emerges from the discussion so far is not so much a number of principles which might help academic staff to work together more effectively. It is rather a series of tensions and paradoxes. When we consider the first concern of staff, the concern about vision and direction, we notice that academic staff have to manage the tension between balancing the demands of the wider environment with the concerns about the present and day-to-day work.

The next major concern was that of consultation – or lack of it – and we can see how the input of the strong individual is essential for robust collaboration. The art of working in contemporary universities involves developing the voice of individuals into a complex, but harmonious, chorus. There has to be a balancing of individualism and collaboration.

Concerns about excessive accountability lead to a direct comparison of accountability for staff and assessment for students and the need for staff to have a clear understanding of what it is that they are being asked to do and how they will be rewarded. Balancing accountability with reward represents another tension.

The final major concern is that the academic staff believe that what they do and what they have done for the organization is not valued. To help staff face change with confidence, attention has to be paid to what has been achieved in the past and what there is to build on. There is a clear tension between managing and balancing what is valued in the past with expectations for the future.

In summary, we can argue that when the major concerns of academic staff are considered in the light of literature on student learning and on learning organizations, there emerges a set of four tensions. These tensions have to be skilfully balanced if academic work is to become a more rewarding experience and offer more worthwhile outcomes for universities themselves. These tensions can be expressed succinctly thus:

- Balancing the vision of leaders with the reality of staff experience.
- Balancing individualism with collaboration.
- Balancing accountability with reward.
- Valuing the past, preparing for the future.

In no way is this analysis exhaustive. Other tensions can no doubt be observed and developed. But these four clearly reflect the often-voiced concerns of academic staff at all levels of the university structure. In the following four chapters I elaborate and illustrate each of these tensions through a series of case studies.

6

Visions and Missions and Reality

> There go my people. I must find out where they are going so that I can lead them.
>
> (Alexander Ledru-Rollin, French politician)

Introduction

We saw in Chapter 2 that academic staff in non-leadership positions believe that there is limited or misguided vision in contemporary universities. Those in leadership positions, on the other hand, believe that there is a stubborn unwillingness on the part of the ordinary academic staff to change. There may be truth in both positions but taking sides will not advance us. The challenge lies in bringing the big picture as seen by the university leaders into line with the day-to-day reality as experienced by the academic staff. The literature involved is summarized in Table 6.1. How this was achieved in one university, is explored here by means of a case study.

Table 6.1 Visions and missions and reality

Area of concern			
Academic staff in non-leadership roles say:	*Academic staff in leadership roles say:*	*Student learning literature says:*	*Learning organization literature says:*
'Senior university leaders have limited or flawed vision.'	'Staff will not change.'	'Learners need to see the salience of what they are being asked to learn and how they are being asked to change.'	'The needs and strengths of staff, as well as the force of external demands, require attention.'

There is a lot of talk of visions, missions and strategies in contemporary universities and a lot of cynicism about them. They are intended to be tools and aids to assist the university and its people work towards inspired outcomes but, more often than not, these very tools and aids become the butt of staff jokes and a source of frustration and anger.

Visions and missions and universities

The purpose of a vision is to present an image which aligns the main directions of an organization with the key concerns and core values of the staff. The visions should illuminate a future and excite the people who must work towards that future. They should embody the unique dream of the organization and the intellectual and creative challenge at the centre of that dream.

It is extraordinarily hard to create a good vision statement. Those to be found outside universities are likely to sound trite. For example, 'Affordable motoring for the family' was once the vision of Ford; 'Computing power for the masses' was once that of Apple. But these visions worked for the people within the organization. They were the right dream to articulate at the right time. It takes a good knowledge of the organization and its people to create a salient vision.

Visions have nothing to say about the major directions the university will take; this is the task of the mission. Missions are functional documents concerning which aspects of scholarship or areas of professional practice it is most strategic to pursue and how, in broad terms, they will be pursued. The mission statement is likely to emerge from a weekend retreat of senior leaders and, naturally enough, will address the concerns of these senior people. To set such directions is the responsibility of these leaders and the statement will address the concerns of these senior staff. It will likely not seem too relevant to staff whose responsibilities and day-to-day work engages them with students, assignments and classrooms rather than governmental policy and economic trends.

Staff may well see the messages and the directions of the mission as inappropriate or impossible and they may well say so – and those in leadership positions will conclude that here again is evidence that academic staff are reluctant to change even though the world of higher education is clearly changing. This tension between the views of the staff and the university leaders concerning contemporary academic work is at the heart of the fears expressed in Chapter 2. Both ordinary academic staff and university leaders are focused on their own viewpoint and that viewpoint is a legitimate one from their particular position but, when the positions appear to have little in common, then communication breaks down, good working relationships break down, and, ultimately, morale breaks down.

From this perspective, the situation is grave. If, however, we attend to the literature on the learning organizations (see Chapter 4), we see that this literature views the tension between the directions proposed by the leaders, and the reality or concerns of the staff, as a necessary tension. The complaints and concerns of each group are not seen as something which hinders effective growth, rather these complaints and concerns are seen as something essential to that growth. Pascale (1990: 126) argues that change flourishes in a 'sandwich'. There has to be consensus and pressure from both above and from below. Senge (1992) talks in a similar way about 'creative tension'. Creative tension comes from seeing clearly where we want to go and telling the truth about where we are, our 'current reality'. The gap between the two generates a natural tension.

Within the university context, the challenge for leaders is to set a path which is achievable with limited resources – and it must be remembered that the university's biggest resource is its staff. It is the staff who will accomplish or jeopardize the fulfilment of the mission and their concerns cannot be ignored. The relevance of the mission must be explained and negotiated so that it encompasses the concerns of the staff who will, ultimately, make the mission happen or let it languish.

It is especially vital that academic staff in non-leadership positions contribute to the discussion concerning strategies because strategies are the things that the staff will do to deliver the mission and, without staff commitment at this level, the key services of the university and the satisfaction of the staff themselves are at risk. One of the comments of those in leadership positions is that staff would rather complain from the sidelines than get involved in the play and constructively act and comment. No doubt there is some truth in this, just as there is some truth in the statement that students want to be told what to do because they do not want to have to think and take responsibility for their own learning. But this does not mean that those in leadership positions should not work to encourage and support staff involvement and demonstrate through their actions that involvement is what is wanted and expected. Currently, a good many staff are of the opinion that their views are neither appreciated nor attended to. One of the messages of this book is that we, as academic staff, can help ourselves to make a difference. We all want colleagues who will help us to face the challenges and the demands which we confront. If we are prepared to attend to the concerns of our colleagues, as well as to our own concerns, then we will likely be listened to and consulted.

By way of example, let us jump ahead a little and consider an aspect of the case study which is discussed in full later in the chapter. The case study features a university whose mission involves a focus on student-centred teaching and learning. Yet, staff in the university are finding it hard to maintain high-quality teaching and learning by traditional face-to-face teaching methods because there are more students, as well as students from non-homogeneous backgrounds, to cater for. From the start, there seems to be a conflict. How can the university be committed to student-centred learning when the staff have limited opportunity to get to know students? If face-to-face teaching is seen to be central to the university's mission, then there is indeed a conflict – but this is not the case. Student-centred teaching is the focus and, in the contemporary age of flexible delivery methods such as internet communication, e-mail and CD-ROM, a lot of attention can be paid to the learning needs of students without face-to-face contact. So the university, or parts of it, finds ways to move towards more flexible ways of teaching and learning without compromising either the mission or the concerns of the teaching staff who wish to do the right thing by their students.

Our universities and their staff must learn to adapt in this way just as transport companies who used to drive stagecoaches adapted to motorized vehicles. Certainly, some things are lost when a given way of transporting or way of teaching is superseded, but other things are gained and sometimes good things from the old ways can be maintained.

Argyris and Schön (1978) have much to say about the way of working which attempts to see the alternative point of view and which positions the problem differently with the purpose of discovering a way forward. They call this type of thinking 'double loop reasoning'. It is, clearly, a vital quality for those of us working in contemporary universities.

For now, however, it is sufficient to acknowledge that it is extraordinary difficult for those of us trained in the independent and critical ways of our profession to collaborate towards ends which, at first, appear quite at odds with what we believe in. All of us tend to identify with our day-to-day work rather than with a seemingly more distant mission. We see our job as academic staff as being about the more tangible things which we do each day and which we are probably good at. It is hard to let these things go, even if we are able to recognize and to agree that they are only a means to an end.

In the following case study we will consider a particular university's vision statement and its effect on the staff, and explore the development of a teaching mission and examine how a newly appointed deputy vice-chancellor (DVC) worked to make it a shared mission and encourage as many staff as possible within the university to become involved in thinking through the issues which the new mission raised. Later we will look at how the staff went on, subsequently, to develop teaching strategies in line with the mission and how they were helped to focus on the new strategies and to let go of old ones.

Case study: visions, missions, strategies and the deputy vice-chancellor. Part 1

The university is a former polytechnic. It was realigning its mission to take account of its new university status. It had always seen itself as a vocational institution with close ties with the local community and industry and it had always prided itself on its teaching. But now it believed that it was time for a restatement of both vision and mission. Its number of fee-paying overseas students was growing, and so were the number of students with high-entry scores. The new university saw itself as becoming a more prestigious institution and with a more international focus.

The newly-appointed DVC was keen to make a fresh start with a new university. He wanted to develop a vision statement which would reflect the new aspirations. The old mottos and advertising material had emphasized local ties; the new one must emphasize the increasing international emphasis of the new university. He wanted a statement which would excite and inspire the staff and to achieve this objective he hired an advertising consultant.

After less than two months, he tried to win the hearts and minds of the staff with the vision statement: 'Vocational education for global excellence.' It did not work. Some senior staff argued that it betrayed the local roots of the organization and others at all levels said that they did not know what global excellence meant. It was clear that attempts to inspire through a vision statement had not worked. He accepted the advice of his vice-chancellor who said that it would be wise to get to know the university, its mood and its people a lot better before he tried again. The DVC agreed and moved his focus on to developing the mission.

This DVC had won his new position because of his reputation as a 'people person'. His ability to work with, and get results from, staff at all levels was nationally known. He was keen to demonstrate this ability early in his new appointment and decided that work with the mission and the subsequent strategy afforded him scope to get results. His way of working emphasized that staff at all levels should be given an opportunity and a responsibility for institutional direction and strategy. The DVC reasoned that if teaching and learning were the core business of the university and involved all levels of staff, then this was obviously the first area which should be addressed.

Before the new DVC had arrived, the senior leaders had already developed a mission which emphasized the move towards international as opposed to local stakeholders. This mission flagged an increase in overseas students and indicated the development of more flexible ways of teaching. The DVC's aim was to get staff at all levels involved in the elaboration of this mission statement and for each faculty and, eventually, each course to develop its own strategy for addressing this mission.

It was stressed to university staff that the broad directions for the mission had been established but that feedback, and possibly some modifications, were necessary and that the people best suited to developing the subsequent mission and strategic documents were the people closest to teaching and learning – the university teaching staff themselves. Consequently, an invitation was made to all of the staff to attend one of two separate 'mission development' days. The aim was to hear from the teaching staff. What did the staff see as the major challenges of having a more international focus and of moving towards more flexible ways of teaching? In what ways might the university work to overcome any difficulties?

Things can be said very often, and very clearly, but people will hear what they expect to hear. The teaching staff of this university were not used to being asked to contribute to a mission statement. In universities, as in other organizations, there are accepted and expected structures for information gathering and decision-making. In this university, these structures were partly traditional, collegiate committee-style and partly more modern managerial. The DVC stepped outside of these established structures and asked directly for comment and, perhaps not surprisingly, he got very limited response. Only around 80 (out of around 3000) teaching staff gave any input at all and most of these responses were negative rather than constructive. Some staff argued that the invitation was actually an imposition – coming as it did at a busy time of the year. They felt that it showed that senior staff did not care about them or know how hard they worked and that the new DVC was no different from the rest in attitude.

Most staff forgot all about the event until a couple of months later when a document was circulated. The document was a summary of the mission and of the perceived problems as expressed by the staff who had attended the two 'mission development' days. Each member of academic staff received a copy of the summary and was requested to comment directly to the DVC if they felt so inclined. A response would also be collected at departmental and faculty level and, if they preferred, they could make their input at these levels.

Once again, the academic staff did not believe it was aimed at them. No more than approximately 5 per cent actually gave an individual response and while most heads of department asked for comments from staff not many pushed for them. The comments which did come in, from all levels, were again critical rather than constructive. On the whole, they defended the current practices of teaching and learning rather than attending to the new mission statement and its implications.

The DVC was determined not to give up. At one level, he argued that to engage the staff with the new directions was the only way to achieve the best from them. At another level, he was aware that he must not be seen to have failed. His abortive attempt to create a new vision was still on his mind. To maintain his credibility within the university, he believed that he had to have salient staff input into the mission. But he was under pressure to make things happen quickly. The vice-chancellor was becoming concerned that all this was taking too long and that there was a good deal of mumbling from senior staff that this was all a waste of time.

The DVC took the advice of the vice-chancellor that working with the established collegial culture might at this stage be a useful way to proceed. Through the academic board, he established a special working party called 'The Teaching Mission Working Party'. The Working Party was to redraft the document in the light of input from staff. It had a month to complete the task. The revised document was sent to the DVC three days before the next academic board meeting – and he rejected it. He argued that the new mission statement did not take account of the comments collected from the staff. The DVC said that he would personally sit on the working party to ensure that the comments of the staff were seriously considered. He reported his action to the academic board and promised that there would be a report the following month.

He was as good as his word. A draft document was prepared in three parts. The first part consisted of the original new mission with the major concerns of staff annotated. The second part was the revised new mission with input from the staff highlighted. The third part was an explanatory document which addressed the outstanding concerns of the staff saying why some of the suggestions, most often made by staff, could not be taken up. This three-part document was endorsed, and welcomed, by the Academic Board, and there was a flurry of approval throughout the university. The DVC was jubilant and decided straightaway to push ahead with a teaching strategy.

Another working party of the academic board was constituted. It was a party of five which included the DVC. The aim was to establish the strategies which would help the university achieve the mission. These were university-wide strategies and not the local strategies which would be developed later at the faculty and course level. For instance, this university teaching strategy signalled the introduction of a coherent and cohesive teaching evaluation scheme which would support the mission's aim of world-class standards in teaching. It also signalled curriculum development and renewal procedures which reflected the mission's commitment to a curriculum which was both relevant and up to date.

The working party developed a draft based on the newly-revised mission document. The DVC personally visited each faculty and sought a response. He even encouraged the staff to contact him via e-mail if they wished to put forward additional comments. Overall, there were approximately 70 responses. Over half of these responses represented groups of staff, course teams, departments and so forth, rather than individual staff and the DVC worked out that the response represented approximately 500 of the staff. The DVC was heartened because, on the whole, these responses were much more constructive ones than those received in the original call for comment concerning the mission. The revised strategy document, including many of the suggested changes, was passed by the academic board a couple of months later. The DVC genuinely felt that the university had achieved a significant step forward.

This is not the end of the case study. It is further developed in more detail later in this chapter. But for now, we will pause and consider what might be learned from the case study so far. What did the DVC do that worked and why, and what did he do that did not work, and why?

Don't tell, ask

The DVC in the case study believed that the way to ensure that staff engaged with the new directions was to both request and expect input from the staff. He got some constructive input but only after some early reluctance and, even, then the quality of the initial input was negative rather than constructive. It took time, patience and guidance to get the more constructive feedback he had envisaged.

It is not hard to see parallels in student learning; telling academic staff about this or that scheme or strategy does *not* mean that it has been accepted or understood any more than telling students in a lecture hall about content specific material means that they either understand or will act on the given information. If we are to work at communicating with our academic colleagues then we have to assume, as good teachers assume, that what is said may well not be heard or, if it is heard, it may well not be understood. The best way to help staff come to change their outlook is to involve them and the best way to involve them is to both request and expect their input.

When working with academic staff we are working with a group of professionals who are a lot less used to listening and learning than our students. Students, on the whole, see their day-to-day task as learning whereas academic staff are more likely to see their day-to-day task as telling. When we work together as academic staff, it is useful to remember our professional weakness, that we find it easier to tell than to either listen or learn. If we want our colleagues to learn from us then we would be wise to begin by asking them to tell us, engage their thinking in this way, and work from there.

Work from where staff are – develop their ideas and vision

Shared directions and purpose emerges from personal direction and purpose (Senge 1992: 9) and that is not because people are self-interested and only pursue that self-interest. It is because people's capacity for engaging with an issue is individual and personal. We cannot engage with things which do not touch us. It was essential that the mission encapsulated some of the ideas and ideals of the staff, but that it also helped staff to go beyond their present thinking.

The DVC put a lot of time and effort into visiting the staff within their faculties and, sometimes, their departments. At each meeting he attended, he would spend around ten minutes explaining the mission or the subsequent strategies. He would then take another ten minutes emphasizing why it was important that *all* staff contribute and he began the staff contribution process by asking them, there and then, to spend ten minutes writing down what they believed were the issues. After ten minutes, he spent another half-hour listening to what the staff had to say and he would then invite all the staff to either hand over, or to send to him later, the comments they had made during the session. In this way, he got significant input and discussion going. He was willing to be open and honest and to say that this or that concern was not relevant or reasonable or that it may be relevant or reasonable but that nothing could be done about it. But, on sufficient occasions, he demonstrated his willingness to see the problem from the position of ordinary staff and this strategy gained him a good deal of trust and respect.

Case study: strategies, the dean and the teaching team. Part 2

Let us now return to the case study to look at the university's teaching strategy in more detail. The university teaching strategy was a document which guided the practice of teaching and learning within the university. It did not, however, mandate specific processes. For instance, the university-wide evaluation system advised that feedback should be gathered from a range of different sources, including students and employers, with the aim of improving student learning and achievement, and that there should be documentation of processes. It did not, however, specify how this should be done. The development of specific strategies was given over to the faculties and to the course teams. Each faculty was requested to produce its own document which reflected faculty priorities and strategies for teaching and learning.

The DVC insisted that it was necessary to give staff who would do the work this degree of freedom in order to get them both involved and committed. A good many of them, particularly those with leadership responsibilities such as course leaders and heads of department, wanted more guidance. They knew they had a difficult job to do and wanted more direction on how to do it.

In all but one of the faculties, a working party was devised to give the staff more direction. These working parties generally included all course leaders and sometimes the heads of departments. The aim was to establish faculty goals and more detailed strategies. For instance, in one faculty, it was decided that student feedback would be collected in every subject, once a year, by using the same questionnaire. Another faculty decided to establish detailed procedures for the reporting of findings and actions resulting from those findings.

Generally, the task was seen by the faculties and by the deans as producing appropriate documentation which could be used to inform and change teaching practice at some later date. As the comment below from the dean of architecture indicates, it was essentially an administrative task:

> There has to be documentation to guide the teaching changes when they do come in. This is what I see this exercise being about producing that documentation. It is not an exercise in changing people. It is part of the preparation for change.

In one faculty, however, namely the Faculty of Social Science, a different process was undertaken. The dean of this faculty stated:

> If we are seriously trying to change teaching then we must engage the teachers now. They will not respond well to a being told to execute a teaching strategy for their course which was largely drawn up by those of us not involved in the teaching.

In this faculty, the course teams were given the initial task of thinking about the changes in their courses which would be required in order to be in line with the university's new teaching strategy. The university, as a whole, and the faculty in particular, were increasingly enrolling students with a wide variation both in background and in prior learning. Overall, the faculty would be increasingly working with both local and overseas students at a distance and contributing to subjects and to courses in overseas universities. What did this mean for teaching? What did it mean for the teaching strategy document which the faculty had to prepare?

Exercises which confront the day-to-day practice of teachers are threatening, far more so than exercises which develop ideas for future change. Not surprisingly, there was resistance from the course teams who claimed that they needed help; that they did not have time to be involved; and that they did not believe in change anyway.

The dean had a meeting with each course leader and their course teams. He emphasized that this was their opportunity to have a say about the future of their courses. He arranged for support from the academic development unit of the university and agreed that any other requests for support, including additional time release for key staff, would be considered if this were deemed as essential. The DVC had provided each faculty with a small budget to get the process moving. This dean decided that to pay for the time release for some of the staff was a good way to spend this money.

During the following month, two course teams worked towards an outline for rethinking aspects of their courses, but the remaining two did not. The dean was adamant that all courses should develop their own plan and determine their own future. He sought permission from the DVC to take a little longer. This was not difficult to achieve – though the vice-chancellor let it be known that he was not impressed.

The details of events in the faculty were as follows:

- The dean's initial chat and offers of support had been enough to get two of the course teams working. With the assistance of the academic development unit and some time release for one member of the team, they had come up with a plan for change and for the necessary processes to follow through with that change. The teams were anxious about their new work but, on the whole, eager to further develop and to try out the schemes which they had discussed. The dean believed that these teams would make significant and worthwhile changes which would result in improved student learning.
- A leader of a third course team produced a document but this appeared to be without reference to other members of the course team. The course leader claimed that nothing significant had come out of the meetings with the team and, consequently, he had composed the document without the team members. The dean insisted that a plan had to come from the whole team and that the leader should try again to involve the whole team.
- The fourth course team had struggled but not progressed.

How the dean worked with these problems and what can be learned from this is explored below in relation to some of the relevant literature which was identified in Chapters 3 and 4.

Defuse defensive routines

In Chapter 4, we saw how Chris Argyris and Donald Schön (1978) identified what they labelled 'defensive routines'. These are particularly common amongst professionals and senior staff in organizations. Argyris and Schön argue that defensive routines work to block learning. They are a major problem which can be identified again and again when professional people are expected to change. These defensive routines involve individuals focusing on errors or problems in the environment around, but never considering themselves, or their own behaviour, as a problem. Argyris and Schön use the terms 'single-loop' and 'double-loop' learning to explain this phenomenon.

- *Single-loop learning* is basic problem solving whereby the goal is external and people work to meet that goal. Academic staff and their leaders are actually very good at this type of learning. It is, after all, the learning which dominates the world of educational institutions and the acquiring of academic credentials. But because professionals are very good at this sort of learning, and because they do rarely experience failure, they have an additional problem – they are not experienced at learning from failure. So whenever their single-loop problem solving learning strategies go wrong, they become defensive, screen out criticism and put the 'blame' outside of themselves. As Argyris and Schön point out, this means that the ability to open up to learning closes down at the very time when it is most necessary to open up the ability to learn.
- *Double-loop learning*, on the other hand, involves opening up to criticism and discussing concerns and alternatives. It means learning from others how they see the situation and admitting imperfections. It also means trying to see the problem in another light, letting go of blaming, and focusing on working positively to bring about satisfactory resolutions.

Leaders and staff can be committed to change but being able to adopt double-loop learning and gain insight from it when they are at their most vulnerable, when their usual strategies are failing, takes more than ordinary commitment. It takes recognition and understanding of the mechanisms at work. Argyris and Schön explain these mechanisms in terms of 'theory in use' and 'theory in action'. They argue that we have a set of theories which underpin our actions, a set of rules which are designed to guide our individual behaviour. This is what we espouse, this is how we claim to act. In fact, we quite typically work by a different set of rules. This 'theory in use' and 'theory in action' explanation has been tested in a large number of empirical studies. The argument is that there is a basic human tendency, in both professional and business situations, to act according to four basic values:

- to remain in control;
- to maximize winning and minimize losing;
- to suppress negative feelings; and
- to be as 'rational' as possible – that is, to define objectives and to evaluate behaviours in terms of whether or not the objectives are achieved.

The purpose of these values is to avoid embarrassment or threat or feeling vulnerable or incompetent. The result of having these values is that people, particularly professional people, go into a situation much more concerned about maintaining their face and avoiding unpleasant exchanges than about listening to their colleagues and learning from them. But they never see this because they assume that they act according to their espoused values and they never get down to examining their actual values in action.

In the context of the case study, the 'theory in use' and the 'theory in action' explanation can be used to address some of the problems experienced by the dean and his faculty. We will examine a meeting which was held between the dean and the two course leaders who had not been able to fulfil the set task. The dean wanted to know what had gone wrong and what could be done to help the course teams. He wanted a plan for future action. The course leaders were far more concerned to defend their lack of success. They were adopting the classic defensive strategies; they firmly believed the fault did not lie with them. They itemized all the reasons why the exercise had not, and could not, and would not, succeed. They pushed blame on to the circumstances and the individuals outside of themselves such as their team members, the lack of time, the countless other tasks and so forth. When the dean pushed the point that something must be able to be done to make it happen – it was clear that neither party was listening to the other and that this particular conversation was going nowhere. It was, however, agreed that the dean should, subsequently, meet with the course teams and listen to what they had to say.

When the dean later met and worked with the course teams he faced a double dilemma. He had the negative feelings of course team members to deal with. There was no doubt that the team members were not happy about having this additional task to complete, but the dean also had to contend with the negative feelings of the course leaders. They had a vested interest in seeing the exercise not work because they had not been able to get it to work.

The first task, as perceived by the dean, was to give a reason why the exercise might work now but had not worked previously. He emphasized that his senior rank made it easier for him; also there had been a little more time for staff to think about and to work on the issues.

The second task was to defuse the defensiveness of the team members. The dean accomplished this by acknowledging the pressures that the team members were labouring under and requesting them to tell him about these pressures. The dean halted the conversation after half an hour, but he took notes of the concerns which were expressed and addressed some of them directly and pointed out how a number of these concerns could actually be picked up during the rethinking about the methods of teaching the course.

After this, the dean, with the help from the academic development unit, undertook a workshop exercise. The aim was to help the staff to clearly articulate the problems which they were experiencing with the existing courses and to explore the ways in which a move towards more flexible modes of teaching and towards more student-centred teaching might address these problems. The exercise worked well with both teams and course leaders becoming engaged with the problems they faced in changing the course and with suggestions of possible ways forward. They were a long way from a final plan, but they had at least begun to engage in a more positive fashion with the problems. The dean was hopeful and with good reason. One month later, both teams produced a draft document. It had been hard work but everyone, even the course leaders, agreed that it had been worth the perseverance.

Argyris and Schön argue that if organizations or groups within organizations want to step out of the defensive routines which so much hamper effective professional practice, then they must receive specific help and training and they must work at it as a group. People can be helped to recognize the reasoning they use when they act and the inconsistencies in their espoused and actual theories of action. It is a challenge, both a personal and an institutional one, but it is one which has to be addressed if significant learning is to be achieved by professionals within the organization and by the organization itself.

Change ways of seeing

This chapter is about balancing vision with reality, but it is difficult to do this balancing if the ideas conflict with established wisdom. Senge (1992) suggests that underpinning all our views and actions are pictures of how things should be and we work to preserve these pictures or 'mental models'. In higher education, in particular, long-cherished ideas or 'mental models' are certainly being challenged. Who are the students? What should be taught? How should it be taught? How should this be paid for? All this is in flux. When staff are asked to evaluate or revise aspects of their professional practice, it is likely that one or other existing 'mental model' will be threatened.

Senge (1992) and Argyris and Schön (1978) suggest that existing 'mental models' can be changed by helping staff to confront problems in their own reasoning or data collection or analysis. To do this with academic staff, however, is likely to be an exacting task. The business of forming and testing an hypothesis and collecting and weighing the evidence is the bread and butter of academic work. Academics are particularly sharp in dissecting the reasoning and data collection of their colleagues, but they are often a touch churlish about having their own reasoning and ways of analysis questioned.

At another level, however, the challenge of changing the existing mental models is the classic challenge of teaching – particularly at university level (Ramsden 1992). In the student learning literature, it is more usually referred to as changing conceptions. It, characteristically, involves finding ways of helping learners to see that what they thought was the case is not necessarily the case, and of creating opportunities to try and test alternative explanations with reference to new or different ways of perceiving and understanding. It may mean seeing an existing understanding as just one part of a larger picture or it may mean rethinking the whole picture. Testing out, experimentation, observation, reflection and discussion are usual ways of working with a class of students. They work almost as well with a group of academics though probably more tact and more humility are necessary as academics are more likely to be wedded to their particular ways of seeing the world than are the students whom they teach.

In the final part of this chapter, we will explore what changing conceptions of teaching looked like in a small corner of the case study already described above (this case is also examined, but with a different focus, in Chapter 7). Increased flexibility in learning was one of the key points of the new teaching mission. In one of the courses, 'People and the Environment', there was some reluctance on the part of a number of the staff to change the face-to-face contact teaching to a more flexible method involving little or no face-to-face contact between staff and students. For a number of staff involved in this course, the entrenched conception of teaching involved face-to-face contact and, preferably, in small tutorial groups. More flexible methods of delivery were seen to be inadequate because they were seen as being less personal. It was argued that if face-to-face teaching were to be sacrificed then the students and staff would lose the sense of community which develops over the weeks and months of a course and is particularly important during the first year.

There were, however, compelling reasons to change the existing practice and the staff could see these reasons and were able to acknowledge them. Their mental model or conception of what teaching should be was increasingly dissonant with what was either practical or possible. There were increased student numbers (from 80 in first year, three years previously, to 100 in the current first year). There had been no corresponding increase in staffing and there was growing student dissatisfaction with the existing provision.

A number of alternative strategies were discussed with particular focus on the large first-year classes which were of particular concern. The alternative strategies ranged from disbanding all lectures and providing notes and tutorials to disbanding all tutorials and introducing peer-run, self-help groups. Various strategies were followed through by different teachers working with different subjects. The group of teachers on which we will focus was the group which was particularly loath to disband the tutorials. The subject they taught was one which focused on environmental issues. It was one where the teachers firmly believed that the ability to collect evidence and to debate was as important as being merely provided with the factual information. The students had the equivalent of four hours contact per week and the students were expected to study by themselves for at least another four hours.

Through a series of meetings and workshops, the group agreed that the essential needs for the students were that they had the opportunity to collect and to share evidence concerning key environmental issues and to be given the opportunity for debate. It was essential that they had 'conversations' with teachers and with peers about what they had done and why. It was agreed that physical presence may not be necessary for these conversations. Such conversations might be conducted through e-mail or on a bulletin board or on a Web-site. Essential material might also be put on a Web-site, rather than given in printed form. Traditional tutorials might be conducted once or twice during the semester, perhaps as an introduction to the subject and then, subsequently, as an evaluation. Students who found the going particularly tough might request individual, one-off tutorials. Staff would meet informally once a week to exchange problems and concerns and to provide mutual support.

Two teachers in the group felt particularly uneasy. They were concerned that they would not be able to keep track of their 20 students and that the students might not become involved with the subject matter. The teachers also expressed misgivings that the workload would end up being far greater than previously. They were also anxious that they would never really get to know their students and that the students would feel no sense of belonging and the teachers were convinced they would end up giving individual face-to-face tutorials to at least half of the group on a regular basis. Nevertheless, the teachers agreed to trial the scheme for one semester on the understanding that their other colleagues, who felt more optimistic about the changes and more committed to them, would be there to assist. By the end of the semester, these same teachers were converts to the changes!

These teachers in a faculty presentation suggested they had learned at least six major lessons:

1. Students adapt very easily to e-mail and to bulletin board discourse. For at least one-quarter of the students, it was not a novel way of operating. They already communicated via the Web and e-mail.
2. A very real sense of community did develop within the group. Different students took on different roles and responsibilities, both formal and informal, just as they might do in the best face-to-face tutorial.
3. It was not difficult to keep check of student input and to ensure that all were contributing and that discussion and debate were moving in appropriate directions. In fact, it was far easier than in a normal tutorial class where, in a fixed time, less than half of the students might have made any contribution and critical issues might not be raised until the end.

4. Students did like the flexibility of being able to tune in at any time. Some students, perhaps one-third, probably spent more time on the subject than might have been expected from a normal class. No student appeared to have spent less time.
5. It was beneficial for teaching team relationships to have the regular tutors' meeting, particularly during the early stages of the scheme.
6. Students did not take much advantage of the additional face-to-face tutorial. They did organize an end-of-semester party which was face-to-face, where they went dressed to fit the aliases they had adopted during the e-mail exchanges, for example, Mr Excess, Lady Spice, and so forth.

The success of this scheme, and the change in thinking of staff in this subject, had a powerful effect on helping other staff in the department to reconsider their understanding of what teaching involved and to try alternatives. Changes such as the ones described here do not arise from merely telling the staff that their ways of seeing are limited or flawed. These changes emerge from both encouraging and supporting the staff to think through current conceptions and then to try alternatives. It is in the doing, and the reflection, and the discussion that significant and lasting changes occur. As stated earlier, helping the staff to change their understanding of their academic work is very similar to helpings students to develop their understanding of subject matter; only far more tact, humility and patience is likely to be required.

Conclusion

Academic staff complain that there is limited vision in their university and their leaders complain that the staff themselves refuse to change. There is a good deal of blame and bitterness and often inadequate effort at seeing where those at different positions in the hierarchy are coming from and what they might be experiencing. How might this be otherwise?

We know from the student learning literature that learners need to see the relevance of tasks before they embrace them and we also know that it sometimes takes patience and persistence to persuade learners that their engagement is necessary and important. It happens best when leaders also try to engage with the concerns of the staff. The organizational change literature emphasizes that the fusion of top–down and bottom–up concerns can create a fertile climate for change as well as for disillusion and disagreement.

The case study described in this chapter explored how staff, at three different levels of the hierarchy, worked to achieve positive outcomes in a climate of significant change. Some of the key principles that guided action will, hopefully, be of use to others. The main lesson, however, is summarized in a comment of the DVC of this particular case study:

> You have to believe in the staff, your colleagues. You have to believe that they have something to offer and you are right to push them to give it. You have to put yourself on the line for them – anything less and you'll probably not win their trust.

7

Collaboration and Independence

> [the human being] experiences himself, his thoughts and feelings as something separated from the rest – a kind of optical delusion of our consciousness. This delusion is a kind of prison for us, restricting us to our personal desires to and affections for a few persons nearest to us. Our task must be to free ourselves from this prison by widening our circle of compassion to embrace all living creatures and the whole of nature in its beauty.
>
> Einstein (quoted by Senge 1992: 170)

Introduction

Jokes making fun of the arrogant and insular side of academic staff and, in particular, their perceived inability to work collaboratively, are well known in our profession. It was suggested, for instance, that this book be called 'Herding Cats'. Such jokes have an element of truth but there is also a good deal of truth which is overlooked. Although academic staff are very often independent and individualistic, they can, and do, work together most productively. The tension between independence, on the one hand, and collaboration, on the other, and how to achieve this in academic work, is the issue at the heart of this chapter.

In Chapter 2, academic staff argued that decisions were often made with little or no consultation or collaboration whereas those in leadership positions argued that discussion with staff was often non-productive because staff savoured debate and the opportunity to put forward their own point of view far more than decision-making. The picture which emerged was one of academic staff not only resisting direction but also resisting taking any positive action themselves. Table 7.1 summarizes the main arguments of academic staff and their leaders, together with salient advice in the literature.

In this chapter, my intension is to gather both the learning organization literature and the literature on student learning and argue a case which, at

Table 7.1 Collaboration and independence

Area of concern			
Academic staff in non-leadership roles say:	*Academic staff in leadership roles say:*	*Student learning literature says:*	*Learning organization literature says:*
'Decisions are made with little or no consultation or collaboration.'	'Academic staff find discussion more enchanting than decision-making.' 'Changes have to be pushed through. Discussion is non-productive.'	'Learners must engage with the learning task.' 'Learners need guidance as well as independence to learn.'	'Shared commitment, not imposition and mandate, brings about successful change.' 'Independence and self-reliance are essential for collaboration.'

first sight, appears to be contrary to the common sense and, indeed, the experiences of the staff reported in Chapter 2. It is contended that academic staff are potentially very good collaborators, that the independence and individualism for which they are often criticized are essential and valuable qualities for contemporary academic collaborations. But – and this is the crux of the issue – contemporary governance and decision-making in universities cannot depend only on the necessarily reflective and time-consuming practices of effective collaboration. This point will be returned to shortly.

There is a second, related, argument made in this chapter and it concerns overcoming the strong anger which came through in Chapter 2 and endeavouring to think strategically when things do not go our way. In times of change, differences over what constitutes a good way forward will abound. There will *always* be times when we believe wrong or bad decisions have been made and we feel frustrated and angry. But we, as individuals, and our universities as social organizations, will be best served if we think strategically, rather than negatively. We need to consider what we can do in these new circumstances to move things to a more satisfying end. The second part of the case study of this chapter is an example of this. A subject leader finds the opportunity to take up a leadership role which is hampered by a range of events, including the actions of colleagues. For a while, the subject leader is angry and resentful, but then, eventually, she forces herself to think more strategically and, therefore, more positively. She begins to focus on what she can contribute to, and learn from, the challenges which she faces. She refocuses on her own teaching and stays on the sidelines while building relationships and credibility until the time is right to become proactive and to show leadership and to win respect.

This argument for realignment is not an argument for abdicating responsibility. It is, rather, an argument for thinking independently and strategically of how to most effectively pursue those things which matter. The very independence for which academic staff are so often criticized can be put to opportune use when used in this way and aided by a modicum of strategic thinking.

For now, we will return to the issue of collaboration in academic work and examine the part played in this by the celebrated independence of academic staff.

What collaborations are and what they are not

The nature and purpose of collaborations is often misunderstood. Collaboration is collective learning; it is the sort of thing which happens when research teams or working parties fuse well together. Colleagues share insights and knowledge and together move towards a fuller shared understanding. It is *not* a situation where individuals compromise themselves; indeed, they exert themselves, but they do so with the aim of furthering understanding and working towards resolving a shared problem, not exercising their own egos.

Collaboration is appropriate when the issues are uncertain and the task unclear and when those involved have a commitment to move forward and there is some time – weeks or months rather than days – to explore the issue. Collaborations are essential to university work but they cannot account for the vast majority of decision-making in universities.

Most decision-making is routine; this is when the task and the desired outcome are clear and guided by policies and procedures established over time by working parties and committees. It does not, for instance, take a collaboration to sign a leave form, book a meeting room or order a new computer. It may, of course, involve cooperation, working with others where there is agreement on what has to be done to achieve a good outcome, 'You do that, I'll do this and we'll make light of the task'. Cooperation has the potential to be time-saving, rather than time-consuming. There will, of course, always be some individuals who are more social and more willing to work with colleagues than others but, on the whole, cooperation, where means and ends are agreed, is not a major issue in the contemporary university (see Chapter 2).

However, an increasing amount of university work is *not* routine with both process and outcome becoming increasingly problematic. In such cases, consultation or collaboration are essential. Collaboration is time-consuming and consultation is less so. Given that time is almost always at a premium, consultation is probably most often practised and, consequently, most often criticized. A senior staff member collects information and opinion to inform a decision. Often, however, colleagues feel that the process is a sham because the eventual decision taken does not seem to encompass their views.

There is no doubt that some consultations, where the collected information is not seriously addressed, are shams. But consultations are not necessarily shams because they do not address all the espoused views. The intention is to collect information to *inform* a decision, not for those consulted to *make* the decision. The deputy vice-chancellor, in the case study of Chapter 6, consulted concerning the mission and the subsequent strategies. He listened to what was said, and was willing to explain the reasoning behind his decision, but he did not feel obliged to use all the advice he received. To do so would have been impossible as much of it was contradictory.

The individual and collaborations

Academic staff at all levels of the hierarchy pride themselves on their independence of thought. Those in leadership positions, however, often see independence in those whom they lead as a form of isolating individualism. When the act of collaboration is explored, however, we will see that there is some advantage in employing the input of strong-minded individuals who are willing to stand up for their beliefs.

The quality of critical questioning is at the heart of academic competence; it is the quality which allows pursuit of truth in research and should be seen as no less of an attribute in other aspects of academic work. Dorothy Lessing (1986: 71) in *Prisons We Choose to Live Inside* argues that the individual and the individual's independence is a much underestimated source of reform. She argues that it is the independent individual who ensures that integrity is maintained in the workings of the group process. In order for the group to maintain honesty, there must be strong individuals; individuals willing to stand out against the group.

Pascale (1990) makes a different, but equally important, argument for ensuring there are a range of robust individual contributions to a collaboration. He cites a law of cybernetics which is the law of greatest variety (this is a law which Senge (1992) also uses to argue for the virtue of variety). This law states that internal controls must incorporate variety because if variety inside the system is reduced, then the system will be unable to cope with variety outside of the system.

The reason for ensuring the strong voice of the independent individual in collaborations is accordingly twofold. First, such collaborations have more mileage because they are more honest. Secondly, they have more mileage because they will, in the end, come up with more potent outcomes – ones which can accommodate or respond to external challenge and criticism.

Making collaborations work

It is not suggested that the outcomes of collaborations will always be sound. The process of collaborating, like the process of working in a research team or learning in a tutorial or symposium, is an uncertain and challenging one. Collaborations, like any other human relationship, do not lend themselves to strict rules, but equally, like other human relationships, they can be made more effective with guidance. The following headings summarize the wisdom of several respected authors in the area of change in organizations (Pascale 1990; Senge 1992; Fullan 1994; Schrage 1995) and these headings are used in order to explore a case study highlighting collaboration:

- Work with the big issues
- Agreed and defined goals
- Competence and commitment
- Respect and tolerance
- Selective use of outsiders
- Leadership and responsibility
- Consensus is not essential
- Regular communication
- Shared space and tools
- Collaborations come to an end

Case study: collaboration

The collaboration focused on here is part of a larger scenario discussed earlier in Chapter 6. The situation described was that of a former polytechnic which was in the process of realigning its mission to take into account its new university status. The new university had been a vocational institution with close ties with the local community and with local industry. A team of senior staff had developed a reputation for their research into balancing tourism and industry and the environment. Demand for their courses was increasing, and the new university was keen to promote the image of being a leader in these emerging areas.

We focus on a subject called 'People and the Environment' (also discussed in Chapter 6) and examine how the staff in the teaching team collaborated to develop a new way of teaching the subject and how they were able to overcome the difficulties which they faced. This subject attracted increasing student numbers but no corresponding increase in staff. The staff believed that their hard work and success was subsidizing other less viable subjects in the university and this was a contentious issue. Halfway through the year, the first-year teaching team were told, by the head of department, to undertake a serious and thorough review of the subject. The head insisted that rising student numbers meant that the maintenance of the tutorial programme was becoming unrealistic. This was particularly challenging for this subject, for a major aim was to enable the students to develop the ability to present appropriate arguments and respond to comment and criticism of these arguments – and the tutorials were seen as the place where these vital skills were developed.

Work with the big issues

The best collaborations involve big issues – issues we can give ourselves to (Schön 1983; Schrage 1995). There are plenty of big issues in contemporary universities but there is sometimes a reluctance to delegate these big problems (see Chapter 2). The present case study does not display this reluctance; the head of department showed trust and confidence in his course team. He showed interest but he had no desire to take control; however, he did insist on results.

Agreed and defined goals

Often collaborations fail because there is confusion or conflicting ideas about what the goal is and what is getting in the way of achieving that goal. It sounds trite to suggest that goals and issues should be clearly identified but a shared understanding of the key issues is not as common as might be thought – and without such shared understanding, discussion gets nowhere. The way the team in our case study worked to define the exact problem and purpose of their collaboration shows the challenges of such a seemingly simple task.

The first-year course teaching team began meeting weekly with the aim of rethinking their teaching. This was a very general aim. In the early meetings of the subject team, (this comprised all the staff teaching the subject, three lecturers and two tutors), there was a good deal of anger and regret that the student/staff ratio had risen from 80 students and six staff three years previously, to 100 students and five staff at the present time. In fact, these early meetings appeared to achieve little except a venting of anger and regret.

The team was lead by a subject coordinator, Dorothy, about whom more is written later in the chapter. The initial challenge Dorothy faced was to assist the group to move beyond their anger and accusations and define the key issues. During the third meeting, when little progress had been made, she suggested that the group try to map the range of topics raised in terms of whether they were central or peripheral to the main issues. After two hours working together on a whiteboard, mapping and rearranging the subjects raised, the group agreed that the main issues were:

- Students had to develop the ability to debate and discuss key environmental issues.
- Tutorial classes of 20 (100 divided by 5) could not ensure that every student developed this ability.
- The team's major task was to find ways of helping the students to develop this essential ability given the present restraints.

All the team agreed on the first two issues. Areas of disagreement concerned what could or should be done. The mood at the end of the meeting was positive even though there was disagreement. The overall feeling was that the issues and goals had been clarified through the joint mapping exercise.

Competence and commitment

It is easy to overlook the obvious and, in the case of collaboration, the obvious is that teams have to possess a minimal level of competence for the task at hand and they need to be committed to achieving a satisfactory outcome. Michael Schrage (1995: 154) makes the point that no matter how diligent or well meaning – a collaboration of incompetents *cannot* be successful. An additional point is that no matter how competent a collaborator may be, without commitment the collaborator can become, at best, a passenger and, at worst, an obstacle.

Also, collaborators have to be very familiar with the problem to hand. They have to have expertise and insight to bring to the problem or issue and they need to have a strong commitment to work through the issue to a satisfactory conclusion. Sometimes people are invited to be collaborators for political reasons or because they are seen to have a small specialist area of expertise. This is not a good idea. It is possible to get such people involved for one-off information sessions or to seek their specific expertise at appropriate times during the collaboration process. The fundamental problem-solving task of the group is best limited to those with an obvious and vested commitment in making the collaboration work and those with specific experience and competence relevant to the issues at hand.

For instance, in the case study discussed in this chapter, there was debate about involving the head of department as a member of the team and he was invited to the first few meetings. He attended the first, missed the second and third because of other commitments, and the team, subsequently, decided to work without him. He did not have subject expertise; he was not familiar with the taught curriculum in the subject, and he clearly had other commitments higher on his list of priorities. He was, however, invited on a monthly basis to join the group for an information sharing session. He took advantage of this only once but was happy to see and hear that progress was being made.

Respect and tolerance

It is one of the most satisfying of experiences to collaborate with colleagues one likes and whose company one enjoys – but it is not a necessary condition for successful collaboration. There are many examples of successful collaborators who do not appear to get along as friends, for example, Gilbert and Sullivan. James Watson, who collaborated with Francis Crick in the development of *The Double Helix*, wrote of Crick: 'I have never seen Francis Crick in a modest mood' (cited in Schrage 1995: 154).

Friendship is not a prerequisite for collaborations, but respect and tolerance are. Successful collaborators put aside irritations of personality and focus on the task – for when the focus is on the task itself, irritability with colleagues diminishes as their contributions grow. The teaching team in this case study had not previously worked together as a team. They had different backgrounds and experiences of teaching. They were, however, all committed to maintaining debate and discussion concerning the teaching of the subject and the issues involved.

The subject coordinator was a senior lecturer new to the department and new to the subject. She had tutored in a similar subject some years previously but her most recent teaching experience was in lecturing (not tutoring) large first-year classes. She had developed a distance-mode package for the subject in which she had lectured. The other two lecturers in the subject (one male, one female) had both been teaching the subject since its development five years previously. The two tutors were both postgraduate students. One of these had been a student in the subject and had graduated three years earlier. The other had done undergraduate work at another university.

There was initial resentment of the subject coordinator. It was believed that she did not understand the subject as it had been developed in the department. The subject leader, in her turn, felt frustrated with the teaching staff who appeared prejudiced and limited in their view of what the subject could become and how the students would respond. It was not an auspicious start.

The success of defining the main issues to be tackled, however, was an important boost for the status of the subject coordinator and important in improving relationships within the group. On one occasion, when one of the lecturers demonstrated some irritability with the subject coordinator, this lecturer was quietly but firmly, chastised by her long-standing colleague. And when the subject coordinator was impatient with one of the two tutors, she stopped herself, apologized and made comment on the tolerance and respect which had developed in the group and how important it was to maintain this tolerance. This polite and respectful way of working was to characterize the group for the first few months and after this time, relations became less formal, but no less respectful.

During the early days of the collaboration maintaining respect and tolerance was difficult. It is not easy to voice different views as to how an issue should be addressed and to maintain good relations. It is a challenge but it is not impossible.

The coordinator helped the group to appreciate the importance of controlling their personal differences and to focus on the central issues. Only then could their knowledge and individuality be the strength of the working group. The group recognized that their strength as a group was in their variation. There was one individual with experience in learning at a distance. There were others who knew the existing subject (its strengths and weaknesses) very well. There was also a former student with experience of another similar undergraduate subject. This meant that different perspectives and different responses to the situation were to be expected. This was the argument made by the subject coordinator to emphasize the point that having disagreement was acceptable – in fact it was to be expected.

There were basically three different schemes proposed for reorganizing first-year teaching.

1. The first was supported by one of the lecturers and one of the tutors. It involved cutting out all lectures and providing lecture material in either published form or on an internet site. This meant that the two hours usually taken in lecture time could be used as additional tutorial time and, consequently, there could be an additional two tutorial groups, thus cutting down the group size from twenty to fourteen or fifteen.
2. The second scheme, which was favoured by another lecturer, was to introduce peer-run tutorial groups of five or six students. Students would meet weekly and work to an agreed agenda. They would report back to a tutor for twenty minutes every second or third week, to ensure that they were on track. In one version of this scheme, lectures would be maintained, in the other version, they would be substituted with materials.
3. The third scheme was developed by the subject coordinator and supported by one of the tutors. It involved the development of e-mail tutorials. Students would be provided with background papers and set topics and questions and issues for debate and these would be published on a specially-developed subject Web-page. Students would be in groups of fourteen or fifteen and two of the lecturers would take responsibility for two groups. Two or three students would have a weekly responsibility to comment on a set topic – a minimum of 500 words each week. The other students would contribute at least 150 words each week. This could be in response to the materials or in response to the other student responses to the articles on the set topic. All responses would have to be in two days before an established time and date each week. Each week it would be one individual's responsibility to overview all comments for the week and the group tutor would then comment on both the process and the development of the arguments.

The pros and cons of these three schemes were debated. Finally, it was agreed that the third scheme, which was the e-mail scheme, had the best potential for attending to the problems being confronted, but was the most likely not to work because of the lack of expertise in electronic delivery. However, this scheme had the most support from the head of department and it was therefore agreed upon to trial it for one year and to provide appropriate electronic training for all the staff and the students involved in the subject.

The two staff members with the greatest familiarity with using e-mail and Web-sites were each given responsibility for two tutorial groups. This meant the subject coordinator and one of the tutors had a double load. It was also agreed that there should be weekly, one-hour meetings of the whole teaching team to check on problems and progress.

There was no lack of discussion and disagreement during the time these issues were debated but there was always respect for the alternative positions. The eventual decision of the group to adopt the e-mail tutorials was not seen by any member of the group as a compromise. It was seen as a positive way forward for the subject – and there was pride that the group had been able to work towards such a positive outcome. Two of the group, in particular, were concerned at the challenge it made on their personal expertise and, partly because of their concerns, a great deal of detailed planning was done to ensure that both staff and students were trained and supported.

Selective use of outsiders

Successful collaborations are more likely to draw in expertise as required rather than attempt to include this expertise throughout the whole of the collaborative period. If collaborative teams become too large, then they are likely not to work effectively. For instance, in the present case study, no-one in the team had experience in setting up a Web-page and early in the planning process the team called in an expert from the university's multimedia unit and sought advice and guidance. The expert did not remain a permanent member of the team, but was involved in briefing the team about the opportunities and limitations of working in the proposed fashion and in eventually setting up a Web-page for the subject. He worked closely with the team in designing the initial training sessions for both the students and the staff and, during the first year of the trial, he continued to work in a consultant capacity.

Leadership and responsibility

Issues of responsibility and leadership within, and around, collaborations are confusing. There are observations in the literature (for instance, Senge 1992; Schrage 1995) that collaborations do not have leaders and followers and yet every group clearly does have a formal leader with a responsibility to report up the hierarchy on developments and often this person will have a formal responsibility for implementing and following through with the decisions of the group.

A distinction needs to be made concerning the work going on within the group and responsibilities outside of the group. Within the group, each member works as an equal. Sometimes the formal leader may take the lead, sometimes other members of the group may do so. But each member of the group is part of the group precisely because he or she has a personal commitment to move the process forward. It is this which the process of collaboration depends upon. Collaborations *cannot* be mandated; they have to be committed to.

In this case study, the subject coordinator clearly took the lead in the early stages of the collaboration, but at other times others did so. For instance, the two tutors took the lead in arguing for, and eventually collecting, feedback from students about the proposed alternatives. They did it because they were intensely involved in the issues central to the collaboration. Their previous experience and expertise made them the obvious leaders of the moment and made them well able to win the trust and confidence of the rest of the team. It is interesting to note that no-one complained about the amount of time it took even though most of the staff spent upward of five hours a week on the task. Like students, academic staff tend not to complain about workloads if they find the work engaging.

Consensus is not essential

Consensus is *not* at the heart of collaboration. Collaborations are about learning collectively, about putting forward a range of options and moving towards an agreed position; they are creative processes which throw up a range of ideas and insights. They are not about everyone within the group coming to an agreement on all the issues being debated and, for better or worse, external circumstances are more likely to influence key decisions than is consensus among collaborators.

In the present case study, there was consensus on the aim; consensus on what was at the heart of the issue and the general direction to be taken, but there was no consensus concerning the strategies which might be developed in order to resolve the issue. Several alternative strategies were put forward and each one might have been successful. The decision to take the e-mail tutorial option was swayed by the head of department who felt that an electronic solution would support the vision of the course as being at the cutting edge. Habitually, external circumstances or politics will move collaborations in one direction rather than another regardless of what issues are under consideration, be it atom bombs or changes in university teaching. Collaborators can put forward a range of possibilities and can suggest preferred options; they can be influential but they cannot guarantee outcomes.

Regular communication

Collaborations, like anything else worthwhile, involve time (usually lots of it) and frequent meetings and communication. Collaborations are exercises in joint creation and the ideas have to be kept alive and humming through regular meetings and communication. But the success of the meetings will vary according to the ebb and flow of ideas rather than the passing of time. Meetings are scheduled and, by necessity, have to be scheduled because the rest of our lives are organized this way, but sometimes the group does not spark and little is achieved and the meeting might as well close early. On other occasions, things move more productively and meetings go on beyond appointed finishing times. Occasionally, individual members of the group have a significant idea and need to discuss it with the other members of the group outside of the established meeting times.

Communication within a collaboration is now wonderfully supported by modern electronic technologies. Ideas in either word or diagrammatic form can be readily e-mailed to the whole group and reactions to these ideas can be expeditiously returned. This is certainly the case with research collaborations. A message is e-mailed or faxed to a collaborator on the other side of the world and comments are back, depending on the time zones, within the day. For many of us, there is no substitute for personal meetings – they appear essential for the development of trust and commitment within the group. Nevertheless, modern communication technologies are clearly supporting our ability to be creative collaborators and should be utilized.

Successful collaborators often develop specialized patterns of communication appropriate to their relationship and to the task in hand. In the present case study, meetings were initially arranged for an hour over the lunch-break – and they did not work. The team felt that they hardly had time to get focused before one or other of the team had to leave. Progress was uninspirational and slow. Consequently, the meeting times were switched to late afternoon (5.00 p.m. onwards) when there were few other pressing demands. The meetings then ran for at least two hours and often continued over dinner and a drink. This added socializing also helped to improve the group dynamics.

These weekly meetings, however, were not the only time during which the members of the team were in contact with one another. They e-mailed each other regularly with questions or comments. During the implementation year which followed, the use of e-mail contact between the team members became even more important as they shared comments on how their tutorial sessions had gone and what they saw as emerging issues.

Shared space and tools

Many of the rooms inhabited by academic staff have whiteboards. It is interesting to observe that most business offices do not. These whiteboards are not just used for seminars or tutorials with students; they are used as collaborative tools when working with colleagues. The best of collaborative experiences will usually have a shared space where ideas or diagrams or other aspects of salient data are jotted down and considered and structured and manipulated. The whiteboard is a convenient means of displaying very simply a developing representation of where the group is at in its thinking and the introduction of the electronic whiteboard has meant that a complete record can now be kept on how ideas have developed over time.

Often collaborations, and indeed learning itself, are thought of in terms of conversations, but conversations, in themselves, are not enough; they merely flag the thinking processes – not the outcome itself. Schrage (1995) has suggested that conversations are rather like bubbles which float around and evoke interest and comment but then pop and disappear. If there is a shared space where ideas can be represented, then the ideas are captured and held and can be, subsequently, manipulated. A diagrammatical representation is necessary in order to keep the group focused in its thinking. As well as this, a shared space discourages self-consciousness on the part of some members of the team and posturing on the part of others. A shared space shifts the focus of the meeting from the comments and positions of individuals to a representation of the shared and jointly-owned ideas of the group and enables the group as a whole to keep their focus on the important issues.

In the case study of this chapter, it was an exercise on the whiteboard which helped the team to clarify the central issues and the desired outcome and helped the team to remain focused on the agreed issues. Let us recall the situation from earlier in the chapter. After two hours working together on a whiteboard, mapping and rearranging the issues raised, the group agreed that the central issues were:

- Students had to develop the ability to debate and discuss key environmental issues.
- Tutorial classes of 20 (100 divided by 5) could not ensure that every student developed this ability.
- The team's major task was to find ways of helping the students to develop this essential ability given the present restraints.

Collaborations come to an end

Collaborations are formed for a specific purpose and once this purpose has been achieved then the reason for the collaboration ceases. Research teams and task forces are fine examples of this, whereby academics come together and focus on specific problems which require to be addressed and once this purpose is completed, the academics then move on to other problems and other collaborations. If the experience has been a good one, the group members may decide to stay together to address other issues, but, essentially, a recasting of the group is required for the group to be effective for a new project.

It must be stressed that the more enduring relationships of departmental or teaching teams should *not* be seen as forms of never-ending collaborations. Such teams will need to work *cooperatively* on day-to-day issues but, when it comes to addressing particular problems and issues, then specific collaborations will need to be formed around these problems and issues and the purpose of the collaborations will need to be affirmed. The practice of committees establishing subcommittees to work on particular problems and issues is part of this tradition.

In the case study, the teaching staff from the 'People and the Environment' subject ceased to collaborate after one year of teaching the subject in the new way. They had developed the new subject and they had trialed it and it was no longer necessary for a problem-solving group to exist around the subject. One of the tutors and one of the lecturers moved to other universities. The subject continued to be taught in the same flexible manner but with new staff. The coordinator maintained responsibility for the subject but took what she had learned to another subject team and began developing a similar method of working.

Naturally, there is a sadness in the idea of collaborations coming to an end, but it is a bit like children leaving home; it is both sad and liberating. It reaffirms what has been emphasized in this chapter, that people are primarily individuals and it is the variety of individual contributions which give a robustness to the collaborations. Group members grow and change through collaborations and, as a result, may need to move on. There are some exceptions, of course, but they are rare.

Independence

At the beginning of this chapter, two arguments were put forward concerning both collaboration and independence. The first, discussed above, was that independence is a necessary condition of collaboration, and the second, which we now address, is that independence in university staff members allows them to work by themselves, if necessary, towards a personal, but professionally relevant, outcome without constant supervision.

In the challenging and changing times currently being experienced by university staff, it is tempting to succumb to feelings of powerlessness. There seems to be so much which appears to be working against us and those things we value. And it is precisely when individuals feel that they have no control over circumstances that they move closest to depression as highlighted by Shirley Fisher (1994) in her book *Stress in Academic Life.* But no matter what is going on around us, and how powerless we feel, we can control how we *respond* to the situation. Michael Fullan (1994) in *Change Forces* tells us that we can choose to learn and grow in the face of change or we can try to shut out the changes and thereby become isolated and resentful. It is not really that the system is out to get us (though sometimes that is the way it seems) rather, it is that the system is merely indifferent to our purposes. Fullan quotes Csikszentimihalyi who states that:

> The primary reason it is so difficult to achieve happiness centres on the fact that, contrary to the myths mankind has developed to reassure itself, the universe was not created to answer our needs.
>
> (Fullan 1994: 7)

No matter what is going on 'out there', an opportunity always exists for both growth and learning. Fullan (1994: 212) again quotes Csikszentimihalyi who suggests that it is those people who are prepared to work with self-contained goals when circumstances are 'brutish and nasty' who will find most satisfaction and achieve most.

Fullan (1994: 133) states that with all the emphasis on team work, collegiality and collaboration, it is vital not to neglect the necessity to both think and act independently, the capacity to be alone and to reappraise the significance of events or directions and to set new personal goals; also to become emersed in new activities, to enjoy the immediate experience, but also to remain aware of what is happening in the larger context – this is how Fullan suggests that individuals need to respond.

These ideas will be illustrated through a story which emerges out of the case study cited earlier in this chapter concerning collaboration. This story focuses on the subject coordinator (Dorothy) who was a senior lecturer new to the department and new to the subject of 'People and the Environment'. Dorothy had tutored in a similar subject some years before, but her most recent teaching experience was in developing a distance-mode package for teaching the subject in which she had been lecturing at another university. The other two lecturers on the subject (one male, one female) had both taught the subject since its development five years previously. One of the two tutors was a postgraduate student of the course. The team were initially hostile because they felt that Dorothy did not understand the subject or the students.

In addition to the professional situation, Dorothy had left an unhappy marriage and her eldest daughter, now a university student, in a city at the other end of the country. A second (15-year old) daughter reluctantly moved with Dorothy. Dorothy had no friends and limited financial resources. She had moved to a tenured senior lecturer position to try to establish her academic career, and to restart her personal life, but the problems she was currently experiencing in settling her daughter and being accepted by her colleagues meant that, what had initially looked like a wonderful opportunity, increasingly looked like a mistake. Dorothy explains:

> I had always thought of myself as a confident and competent woman. Within a month, my image of myself had plummeted to such a level that I was on the brink of genuinely believing that I couldn't cope by myself and that I should go back. It was fear of looking foolish that stopped me – not my own resolve to stay and work things through.

Dorothy agrees that for over a month she did little but despair and feel sorry for herself then, after her 15-year-old daughter had been returned to her after running back to her father for the second time, Dorothy describes how she started to take control:

> I realised that I had to find something positive in the situation and, if I couldn't, then the positive way forward probably was to resign and go home.

Below, we explore how Dorothy went about finding something positive in her situation.

Set personal goals

It is extraordinarily difficult to turn away from goals and ambitions which might be blocked or no longer relevant and to develop new goals and ambitions. On the other hand, to stay committed to what can no longer be pursued breeds a good deal of resentment and frustration, and very little which is either productive or satisfying. In the interviews in Chapter 2, there were a good many men and women who exemplified this point. Their bitterness may, at one level, have been justified but there are no winners in the game of standing out against inevitable change in contemporary university work. This is not to suggest that we simply give up and switch routes in an unprincipled way at every hiccup. Chapter 6 discussed the importance of being clear about the principles which underpin our work – and returning to those principles for guidance. For instance, if student learning is our concern – then we may need to sacrifice face-to-face tutorials – to do so is not unprincipled because there are other ways of assisting students other than face-to-face tutorials. This is not to advocate an arbitrary choice of new directions but when circumstances change so much that the old goals are no longer attainable, it is not productive to dwell on them, though to switch direction, especially without assistance, requires considerable courage and independence.

Dorothy explained that she had had great expectations of the new job and had faith in her ability to be able to make a difference both to the subject and the department. She had felt well equipped with knowledge and experience and genuinely believed that she had a good deal to offer. She had originally seen herself as a leader but in the current circumstances, where she felt resented and where there was no trust or acceptance of her background or ability, she was unable to adopt a leadership role. She did the necessary administrative tasks but, academically, she did not lead the group.

The new goals Dorothy set herself were related to her teaching. She concerned herself with helping the students to learn, enjoy and engage in the subject matter and to developing her own understanding of how what was taught at her current university differed from her previous experiences of teaching the subject.

Become immersed in new activities

Once focused on the teaching and the students, Dorothy quickly began to feel better. She had always felt that she was a competent teacher and she genuinely enjoyed working with young people. She was committed to the subject and knowledgeable about it. She was obviously a success with the students; she enjoyed the classes she took and was happy to take on any additional classes when there was sickness among the other staff members.

Enjoy the immediate experience

Because she had limited social opportunities, Dorothy put a lot into, and got a lot out of, the teaching. She organized a couple of field trips and some social events. She told herself she may never have such a good opportunity to devote herself to her classes – so make the most of it – and she did. (Her students, subsequently, put her forward for a good teaching award.)

Remain aware of what is happening in the larger context

Dorothy's success as a teacher began to win her respect from her colleagues. This was not the reason she had focused on teaching, but once she became aware that she was becoming increasingly accepted, she began to adopt her leadership role. The case study shows the expertise which she was eventually able to bring to this leadership role.

Dorothy finally achieved her original ambition of developing significant authority in her course leader role and of developing the subject and her own leadership abilities. She did not do this by giving up and despairing when the context appeared unsupportive. She did it by showing that she could operate effectively irrespective of those unsupportive aspects of the context. She displayed an ability to be able to set personal goals despite the circumstances and focus on them and learn and grow and find satisfaction and enjoyment as a teacher. When the external environment was more propitious she was aware enough to make a move and take on a genuine leadership role.

Summary and conclusion

In Chapter 2, academic staff complained that there is little or no consultation or collaboration. Those in leadership positions, however, are concerned that the staff often savour discussion and debate more than decision-making and that their involvement in decision-making would mean long, protracted negotiations. We have argued that consultation need not be time-consuming. Opinions and information can be collected quickly and efficiently and consultation informs action; it does not dictate it. Having said this, if consultation is to be seen to have integrity, there must be explanation as to why certain decisions have been taken and why alternatives were not. Staff have to believe that their voice has been seriously considered, and also see that sometimes their opinions are attended to.

Collaboration is different to consultation. Both are time-consuming, but they are also extraordinarily useful. They are joint learning ventures which have the potential to build morale as well as develop new insights and ways forward. Academic staff, because of their independence of thought and their inclination not to go with the flow, are particularly good at standing out against quick fixes and developing robust and salient collaborative outcomes. But collaboration, like so much of learning, needs guidance.

Finally, in this chapter, it has been argued that the characteristic independence of academic staff not only assists us to undertake worthwhile collaboration, that is, collaboration which results in significant developments in understanding, it also allows us to focus in and find personal relevance and satisfaction in our work – even when much around us is far from supportive or satisfying.

8

Accountability and Reward

> The promotion round was a lottery. What else could it be when those sitting on the panels knew less about teaching than those who were applicants?
>
> (University lecturer)

Introduction

In Chapter 3, it was proposed that what is assessed in a subject or course shows what is truly valued – and that this is what students work towards. Frequently, there will be a mismatch between the rhetoric of what is claimed to be of value and the reality of what obtains good grades in assessments, but students quickly work out the truth and academic staff are no less keen to work out what is really valued and rewarded in academic life. Typically, they see these rewards going for research and, sometimes, outstanding teaching, but they see few rewards for attending to the mechanisms of accountability. They remain dismissive of schemes which tie up their time in this way, and yet the success of the university, as a whole, depends on its demonstrated accountability. The challenge, at least in part, is to link the accountability mechanisms of the university itself with the schemes of personal recognition and reward of the academics themselves.

The arguments of academic staff around the issues of accountability and reward, together with relevant guidance from the literature is summarized in Table 8.1.

Accountability

It was argued in Chapter 2 that the implications of a bigger, and consequently more costly, higher education sector was more accountability. No government is likely to invest substantial and increasing amounts of money

Table 8.1 Accountability and reward

Area of concern			
Academic staff in non-leadership roles say:	*Academic staff in leadership roles say:*	*Student learning literature says:*	*Learning organization literature says:*
'Excessive scrutiny and accountability gets in the way of real work.' 'Accountability is not linked to recognition and reward.'	'Accountability exists at all levels of university work. We are now all accountable.' 'Accountability has advantages – some staff need to be made more accountable.'	'Assessment must link to desired learning. Desired learning must be what is rewarded and recognized.' 'Assessment processes must support not get in the way of desired learning.'	'Develop organizational structures which support and reward the desired learning processes and outcomes.'

without first ensuring that there exist ways to check how the money is being used. Over the past few years, universities have bolted accountability into the structure and fabric of their organizations. They have worked hard to show themselves to be responsible and responsive, efficient and effective and academic staff have expressed concern about such developments. A good many have argued that this heralds the end of traditional academic freedom (see, for example, Marginson 1997) but if we look back to the interviews with academic staff in Chapter 2, we see that staff do not necessarily see accountability, in itself, as a bad thing. There is often general acknowledgement that it is necessary and may even be worthwhile. The major concern is that the systems which are created around accountability get in the way of the real work of teaching, research and scholarship and that there is too much accountability and too little support, reward and recognition (as reflected in the opening quote). The following comment captures the concerns:

> Accountability is separate. It has little to do with the main business. There are special reporting mechanisms; there's a special language which relates to aims and objectives and outcomes but the main business itself, the teaching, the projects, the problems we explore, the anguish of exploring them, and the learning that goes on in the process – all of this is missed. No reward or support or acknowledgement goes for attending to this, and yet this is what it's really about. So we have this time-consuming activity which takes hours to complete which really fails to address the thing it purports to be concerned about.
>
> (Senior lecturer, social science)

Many of us will have heard students say similar things about poor assessment – it gets in the way of learning; it deflects from significant and engaging issues; and directs attention to the trivial (see, for instance, Ramsden 1992: 67–8). We saw in Chapter 3 that this sort of assessment was associated with surface approaches to learning and there is ample evidence both in the survey reported in Chapter 2, and elsewhere (see, for instance, McInnis 1996) that poor accountability procedures encourage the same type of superficial responses in academic staff. Just as assessment procedures need to build on, and contribute to, the learning which is central to the course, so accountability must build on, and contribute to, learning and development which is at the heart of academic work.

There are two other related issues to pay attention to. First, reporting mechanisms must not be too cumbersome; documentation is necessary but must not be weighty. If staff can see the point of the documentation then they will usually do all that is necessary. If they cannot see the point, then no amount of additional documentation will make the exercise more meaningful. There are a good many well-meaning schemes which have floundered because of overburdensome reporting mechanisms (Reeders *et al.* 1996). The second consideration (and this takes us back to a key issue of this chapter) is that the accountability mechanisms must tie into schemes of personal recognition and reward for the academics themselves.

Documenting achievement

Many readers will be familiar with the argument that promotion schemes in universities reward research a good deal more than they do teaching. There are a range of related suggestions as to why this is so (Ramsden and Martin 1996). One of them is that teaching is considerably more difficult to document than is research. The indicators for research performance such as research grants, published work in academic journals or books, and citations by other authors, are relatively easy to document. Teaching, on the other hand, is much more challenging in this respect. All academics are expected to have taught and somehow it is expected that students will have learned. But what has been learned and whether the quality of the teaching was really associated with the subsequent student learning is a difficult argument to demonstrate.

Increasingly, there is argument that if teaching is to be valued equally with research, then we must collect more robust evidence that teaching has been undertaken in an effective and scholarly manner and that the students have actually learned as a result of that teaching (see, for instance, Boyer 1990; Ramsden *et al.* 1995). The 'teaching portfolio' becomes the deposit for this information. The collected evidence chronicles how the teacher makes sense of, engages with, and learns from, the professional practice of helping students to learn. If the teacher is at a senior level then it is likely the argument will include how support has been provided to colleagues to assist them to develop as scholarly teachers. The teaching portfolio is, therefore, a record of professional practice and of achievements resulting from this practice. The evidence and documentation which supports the portfolio will likely take up a good many filing cabinets or computer disks and the document itself will likely be a weighty one. As a rule, for promotional purposes, a summary only is required.

A particularly compelling case for the teaching portfolio is made by Edgerton *et al.* (1991: 4) who reason that documentation around the portfolio facilitates improvements in both the learning of students and the learning of staff, not least because systematic documentation, observations and reflections provide significant substance for staff-room discussion about teaching which in turn leads to greater interest and, subsequently, discussions and papers within the larger community of scholars. Finally, and most importantly, teaching portfolios allow teaching to be captured into something more permanent than the bubble of conversation which might occur in the corridor. It allows teaching to be represented and explored in 'substance and situatedness'.

It would be misleading to suggest that the reporting of all teaching is challenging while the reporting of all other academic work is non-problematic. Research in less well-established areas also sometimes needs to be represented and explored in a 'substance and situatedness' not readily captured through the traditional research-reporting methods. That is: what were the particular problems; how were they tackled; what informed them; what resulted; and what is evidence of all this. The reporting of community service, which typically forms the third of the three areas of academic work, is also extraordinarily ill-defined and, therefore, challenging to report.

Ernest Boyer (1990: 34), in his compelling report *Scholarship Reconsidered*, shows that almost 70 per cent of academic staff believe that the academic profession needs better ways of conceptualizing and evaluating scholarly performance than those it currently employs. Boyer's response is to argue for four separate, yet overlapping academic functions, all based on scholarly activity. The first is the scholarship of 'discovery' which reflects traditional research. The second is the scholarship of 'teaching' which involves transforming and extending, as well as presenting, information. The third is the scholarship of 'integration' which reflects the contemporary need to work across disciplines and to communicate the often highly-significant results to a non-specialist audience such as work in the areas of bioethics or environmental science. Finally, the fourth is the scholarship of 'application' which reflects the growing need to apply what is discovered in more traditional research to the problems which arise from practice. Boyer argues for portfolios, very similar to the teaching portfolio described above, to reflect work in all the scholarly areas.

The documentation of achievements within the portfolios will likely make less traditional forms of scholarship more assessable and, therefore, more rewardable within formal university award schemes. But formal reward is only part of the picture. More often than not, the concerns of teachers regarding the lack of reward for teaching, in particular, relate to their perception that they get little feedback or appreciation from senior colleagues and supervisors (Ramsden and Martin 1997). At one level, this involves staff with leadership responsibilities taking an active and informed interest in what is happening in teaching; at another level, it involves giving more systematic or structured support and feedback.

We have argued strongly in Chapter 3 that a vital part of learning involves feedback on progress and achievement. Feedback for students usually comes through assessment. Feedback for researchers comes through peer discussion of conference papers, peer review of the manuscripts which the researchers submit for publication and through the scrutiny of the applications they make for research grants. To some extent, formative assessment for teaching comes from both the learning and the responses of students to questionnaires, but more support from colleagues is needed here. Just as it is hard for students to judge the progress they are making without input from peers and supervisors, so it is hard for academic staff to evaluate their progress and work without similar input. If we want a culture where staff learn, then we need to develop a culture where staff readily assist one another to do so.

This feedback and guidance role is now often formalized in terms of a performance management or workplan and such schemes are sometimes strenuously resisted by academic staff who argue they need no such schemes to help them to perform (Bright and Williamson 1995). Paul Ramsden (1998), in his book *Learning to Lead*, emphasizes that often staff resist such schemes because they see them as externally-imposed regimes with the aim of controlling. If, however, they could be seen as an opportunity for supporting and for creating an environment and situation where staff might enjoy personal success, then they will be more readily accepted. A good scheme supports staff to move in particular directions; it offers opportunities for advancement and learning as well as encouraging alignment with institutional directions. If the learning of staff is to be supported then, as with the learning of students, a context will need to be established. For students, the context is an assignment or learning contract. For staff, it is the workplan.

Performance management might be seen as a second-generation attempt to support and guide academic work. Appraisal mechanisms were the first generation and, on the whole, achieved minimal success (Ramsden 1998). Performance management has a different focus. It looks forward at what can be achieved and how, whereas appraisal tended to look backwards, at what had been achieved and why. Of course, some appraisal schemes looked forward as well as backward and some performance management schemes will likely consider what has gone before as well as what is ahead, but the difference in emphasis is an important one, partly because one is potentially more positive than the other, but also because the key aim – to plan and support the performance of academic staff – must be reflected in the design of forward-looking performance planning. Ramsden (1998), based on Egan (1995), has developed a series of headings to guide the process and these are listed below:

Objectives:	'What key things will I achieve this year in my academic career?'
Delegation:	'What authority do I have to make them happen?'
Workplans:	'What will my supervisor do to help me achieve them?'
Feedback:	'What feedback can I expect from my supervisor?'
Tracking:	'What is the best way of tracking my progress?'
Recognition and reward:	'What recognition will I get for my accomplishments?'
Development:	'How can I prepare myself to do bigger things?'

A shorter, simplified version of this list is used to structure part of the case study which is presented later in this chapter.

The argument made so far is that accountability systems will drive academic work and learning just as surely as assessment systems drive student learning. What is important for the university is that the development of knowledge and learning in both staff and students must be served by, and not threatened by, such systems. The promotion of individual academic staff, which is still the most conspicuous reward system of the university, must link into the accountability system of the institution as a whole, but staff will also need regular and systematic guidance and support to work within the new academic environment. Staff cannot be expected to change and to learn with no guidance or support any more than we might expect our students to change and to learn with no teaching.

Later in this chapter, we explore what this type of support looks like in a case study which depicts an academic department stretched to its limits with change. The department is experiencing a fourfold change. First, it is trying to cope with the introduction of a new quality assurance system; secondly, it is adopting a new process of performance planning; thirdly, it is revamping its major degree course; and fourthly, it is attending to a push to improve research performance through a new collaborative scheme with industry.

The case study

The Department of Industrial Design is situated within the Faculty of Engineering. Its undergraduate course prepares students to work as designers in the manufacturing industry. Graduates gain jobs designing anything from a can-opener to safety equipment for a nuclear-power station but the department has developed a strong relationship with the electrical and electronic industry and the majority of its students find jobs in these areas. The department has eight permanent, full-time members of academic staff and up to ten casual staff, mainly tutors and technicians, who are employed at different times of the year.

The department began its life ten years ago, shortly after the appointment of a foundation chair in industrial design. The appointee, Professor Ronald Simms, had a worldwide reputation and significant research and industrial experience. It was he who pushed for, and developed, the undergraduate degree course. However, after establishing the degree course and teaching it for a couple of years, he had increasingly focused on his research. Over the years, he had won several important and sizeable research grants for the department, mainly involving design for aspects of the nuclear-power industry. After nine years as professor and head of the department, he was attracted by a chair at a prestigious overseas university and he left.

A major concern of the university, and the department, was how to maintain its research record in this area. The head had taken with him a couple of key researchers and the connections with industry were, to a large extent, based on his reputation. The department was temporarily headed by the other professor in the department, Simon, who had a good research record but had no wish to permanently take on the headship role. A new head, Ted, was eventually appointed. Ted had limited academic experience but a strong design background and significant business management experience. Ted was seen as someone who would attract industry support and be able to pull the existing staff together into a strong coherent team, with Simon, the existing professor, leading the research.

The leadership of the undergraduate course was not initially considered an issue. It was assumed to be healthy. There was no problem in attracting students and graduating students had little problem finding employment. The electrical and electronic and nuclear-power industries were all thriving and developing and students always had a clear advantage when applying for jobs in these areas.

This case study is a complex one as there are four separate but interweaving issues to be addressed. The first is the issue of rekindling the department's shrinking research profile. The second is the issue of making changes in the undergraduate course. Linked to these two issues is the introduction of a system of performance management within the department and the establishment of personal portfolios to document performance. All this is happening against the background of the fourth issue which is the development and implementation of the university's quality-assurance scheme. It is a challenging time for this department.

Issue one: research development

When the former head, Professor Ronald Simms, left the department and took with him a couple of accomplished senior researchers, the capacity of the remaining group to attract new research grants and students was seriously threatened. The remaining professor (Simon) and the new head of department (Ted) saw the saving of the department's research reputation as their major priority.

The department had enjoyed positive relationships with a number of major national and international companies. Over the years, however, the number of major collaborative projects that the department and industry had worked on had diminished. Simon explained it this way:

> Initially, we got our reputation from working on a major project designing for the nuclear-power industry and we really outshone some of the American design teams. We were an outstanding group and we did some other innovative things in those early years. But, for a few years now, we've gone along on reputation. Particularly with Ron [the former head of department] gone we needed to re-establish our credentials.

Ted and Simon worked to develop a research-student scholarship programme with three large companies. Through this scheme, up to three research students would each be granted a scholarship and appropriate resources to tackle problems or topics put forward by the companies. The three companies could put forward two topics each for investigation. From a maximum of six topics, three would be selected for investigation by a research student, supported by both an industrial consultant and a university supervisor. A committee comprising representation from all the three companies, the university, and the department would make the final selection of both the topics and the students.

It was believed that this close working with the people and the problems confronting the major companies would help redevelop working relationships with industry and familiarity with their contemporary problems. It was also believed it would attract high-quality research students and provide the staff in the department with the opportunity to get involved in supervising the projects and developing their own relationship with the companies.

The scheme was seen by both Ted and Simon as a considerable achievement. It was not, however, greeted enthusiastically by the rest of the staff within the department. Ted and Simon had mentioned the proposal in a staff meeting or two, but at no time had they sought input or comment from the staff. Ted and Simon had simply assumed that the plan would be seen as a positive by all staff and were surprised when this was not the case.

The concerns which the staff expressed were first that they did not necessarily want to be involved in projects imposed on them by these particular companies; they wanted to pursue their own ideas and links. Secondly, they felt that the department had inadequate space and facilities to accommodate extra research students. The department had six existing research students who shared two rooms and had frequently commented on lack of both space and facilities.

Ted and Simon listened and responded to the comments and concerns of staff as best they could. They invited their colleagues to offer modifications or alternative suggestions. A meeting was arranged for a date in a month's time when such modifications or suggestions might be formally presented. This would allow the staff some time to explore alternatives.

Issue two: the redevelopment of the undergraduate course

The undergraduate course was not, at first, seen as a problem for the department. The course attracted high-quality students who had no trouble finding work in the industry. It came as something as a shock, therefore, to find that student evaluations recently required by the university to be undertaken at each year level, suggested some deep-seated dissatisfaction. In particular, students felt that the content was too removed from the problems of the profession and they wanted more direct experience with real design problems. A quick check with employers indicated that they also supported this idea. The academic staff were less enthusiastic. The team who taught the course believed that it was vital that the students got a good grounding in core discipline knowledge and they stressed that the students could only apply knowledge to problems when they had some basic understanding. However, the new university quality assurance scheme which had prompted the evaluations required that the student dissatisfaction be addressed in some way.

Issue three: performance management scheme

At the same time as all of the above was happening, the department was involved in implementing a university-wide system of performance management for all the academic staff. Ted was very positive about this. He felt that this scheme would help him to get to know his staff much better and enable him to work more effectively with his staff. Ted had had experience with performance management in his previous job.

Ted was convinced that his staff would need a good deal of information and support in order to limit suspicion and enable the staff to see the benefits rather than negatives in the scheme. An information session was organized during which the university's Human Resource Management Group explained the formalities of the university scheme and Ted himself also spoke about his own positive experiences of a similar scheme in his previous job. He also provided a checklist which he had developed for guiding the initial interview with the staff. He used this checklist as a starting-point and asked how it might be changed to be most useful in the current situation. This was a most successful exercise. The staff became engaged with the opportunities which the process afforded and came up with a list which is reproduced below. The list was divided into two parts. The first part focused on what should be covered. The second part concentrated on how the interview should be conducted:

- What should be covered?
  The context as perceived by each party.
  Major aspirations (and disappointments).
  Connections with departmental/university directions.
  Help to be given.
  Feedback.
  Specific objectives.
  Specific indicators of performance.
- How will the parties behave?
  The discussion will be positive and forward-looking.
  Each party will listen and attend to the concerns of the other.
  Each party will commit to seeking a genuine way forward for both individual and department.
  If, upon reflection, either party has concerns about aspects of the interview a further interview will be arranged.

Maria

The interviews with two of the staff, in particular, are highlighted here. Maria was a lecturer in the department and had been there for three years. She had a Master's degree but no PhD. She wanted to undertake PhD work in the area of the design of electronic equipment for people with disabilities. She had a disabled husband and, therefore, she had a personal as well as a professional interest in this area. Maria was also the department's most committed teacher, and was the coordinator of the undergraduate degree. She feared that the proposals to redesign the undergraduate course would mean there would be no opportunities for her to develop her research.

The first interview with Maria did not go well. Despite all the guidelines concerning being positive and forward-looking, Maria could not contain her anger. The way she perceived her current situation was that for the previous three years she had carried a very heavy teaching load. She had been the coordinator for the department's main degree course and also the coordinator of the first year of the course. She had done a prodigious amount of work, but had received little support, reward or recognition during that time and now, under a new regime, this situation was to be perpetuated. She was being expected to redesign the undergraduate course, take on an excessive teaching load and she was not being written into the projected research developments even though she had been very vocal about her area of interest and its importance and relevance.

It was hard for Maria to get beyond her anger in the first interview but, before the interview was terminated, Ted and Maria heeded the last of the guidelines – to call another interview if the first had not proved to be productive. This second interview a week later was much more productive.

By the end of the second interview, it was agreed that Maria's concern about disability design would be taken to the research consortium. Ted agreed that he and Simon would put forward the suggestion that at least every three years one scheme should address an aspect of disability and that

Maria would be involved in this. If an appropriate scheme emerged, Maria, herself, might go forward as a part-time PhD candidate. In the meantime, Maria's teaching load would be adjusted to take into account her involvement with any projects. She would drop her responsibility as first-year coordinator and all her first-year teaching, but she would remain overall course coordinator with the major responsibility for the redesign of the course.

Eric

The next case is that of Eric, a senior lecturer in the department since its inception. Eric had always been on the periphery of activity. He had a particular interest and expertise in environmentally-friendly design. Within the wider, national community, he had a reasonable reputation but his work had never figured prominently in the directions of his own department. He was a rather withdrawn character who rarely talked about or pushed his own specialism. He was, however, a most conscientious teacher. His interest in the environment often found its way into his teaching even though there was no particular subject on environmentally-friendly aspects of design within the curriculum as a whole.

Two initial interviews were also conducted with Eric. The first went for just over half-an-hour with Eric being characteristically withdrawn. He agreed he was not happy with the research scheme because he felt his area of interest would not be considered. The collaborating companies had a track record of ignoring environmental issues, and, as he explained:

> I have spent twenty years trying to get the environment on the agenda. I've got nowhere. It's not going to happen because we have some small-time arrangement with them and that means the work I've done, the things I care about, has no place in the future direction of this department.

At the second interview, Ted suggested some alternatives. He argued that there were three possibilities. First, Eric was invited to sit on the consortium to emphasize the importance of environmentally-friendly design. Attention to the environment was a strategic direction for the university and it was, therefore, appropriate that the issue be pushed at the consortium level. Secondly, Eric would seek one or more companies whom he knew to be more likely to support environmentally-friendly design products and attempt to build a similar research scheme with them. Eric would receive the department's support in this. Thirdly, Eric would focus his concern for environmental design into the rethinking of the new curriculum. It was, clearly, an issue that young designers would have to address in the immediate future and Eric was obviously the person to lead this.

At a later interview, Eric came forward with a suggestion of his own. He would take on the redesign of the curriculum in partnership with Maria and he would take over from Maria as first-year coordinator. Eric was particularly keen to explore the environmental dimensions of design in first year, but he was also keen that these environmental issues not be neglected in later years and he intended to approach companies and ask them to submit real problems for students to work on in second and third year.

Ted undertook all the interviews and negotiated the workplans with all the academic staff. Each plan focused on two or three agreed major areas only. It was to include: objectives and an outline of the main ways of achieving the objectives; special training/development (including conference requests); arrangements in place for receiving feedback from the supervisor and colleagues and the expected outcomes. Ted agreed to meet with each staff member fortnightly to talk through progress and frustrations and, where appropriate, to provide feedback.

How the staff developed ways of documenting their plans relates to another of the issues raised by this case study.

Issue four: quality assurance at the university

The university was introducing a major quality-assurance scheme which involved documenting and reporting on the three major areas of university activity: teaching, research and community service. In terms of teaching, each course had to be evaluated at every year level, and each subject within the course had to contribute to the overall evaluation. The feedback from the evaluation had to be summarized and, appropriate action, in terms of changes or further enquires, had to be documented. For both research and community service, there was a requirement of regular evaluation, documentation and reporting which had to be undertaken for each major project. Each course and each major project would be reviewed every three to five years by a team which would include one member external to the university.

The university scheme set down these basic guidelines but left the detail to be developed within the departments. Overall, the university was experiencing resistance in trying to convince the staff that this documentation of work was a useful and necessary way to go. The Department of Industrial Design was better placed than many of the other university departments in winning the support of its staff. Many staff members had worked in an industrial setting where such documentation was common; their main concern was how much time and effort the scheme would consume.

The academic staff met over two or three weeks to develop departmental guidelines for documenting teaching and course and subject development. They readily agreed the following:

- All progress reports be no more than one page long (but that year-level reports should include subject reports as an appendix and full course reports should include the year-level reports as an appendix).
- Reports be made available for discussion annually at a special staff meeting.

- Reports be supported by documentation, e.g. minutes of meetings, memos, etc. to be available on request.
- Changes in teaching activities must be supported by evaluation of existing practice by students and others, e.g. educational experts, employers, colleagues. Evidence must be available but need not be submitted.
- Where appropriate, documentation and reports be included in the teaching journals and summarized portfolios of individual staff members.

Personal portfolios: linking individual and university goals and demonstrating accountability

At this point, Eric and Maria are again drawn into the case study. Both had hoped to apply for promotion within the near future and both believed that they had done a lot and deserved promotion but they felt that they did not stand out as compelling candidates in conventional academic terms. Neither had a strong publications record and neither was confident about being able to present the worthwhile work which had been done in a convincing form. Ted (the new head of department) agreed that, as part of their performance plans, Eric and Maria should work to develop their own portfolios but also develop draft guidelines on promotion portfolios for all the academic staff. The university was about to review its promotion procedures. Teaching and community service portfolios were an issue to be addressed by the review panel which was to decide whether or not the university should insist on the teaching and community service portfolios for promotion and, if so, what they should look like. Ted was a member of the academic board subcommittee which would undertake the review.

Both Ted and Maria wanted to develop a combined portfolio which would assist the staff to document and to present evidence concerning all aspects of their academic work: teaching; community service; and research. They suggested that it be called their academic work portfolio. Maria explained that her commitment to designing for disability affected all aspects of her work. For instance, in her teaching, she availed herself of the current research in the area and encouraged her students to consider the area in terms of their own design. She then passed on her expertise and insights developed through teaching and research in her community service. There was also her personal commitment in the area given her husband's disability. It was both efficient and sensible to document all of Maria's work in similar ways because there was so much overlap.

Ted advised caution as he was aware that, at least in the short term, the criteria and standards concerning promotion on the basis of research were unlikely to change within the university. He was also aware that many staff members did not have such an integrated approach to their work as did Eric and Maria. Nevertheless, Eric and Maria pushed their case and argued that it was in the university's interest to develop a more integrated approach and that the university staff be seen to relate one aspect of their work to another aspect of it. Eric and Maria maintained that their draft portfolio would not undermine the traditional ways of documenting research but, rather, would help to document the work of those involved in research of a less conventional and more applied nature.

A compromise was reached. The system was to have a project focus. Projects would be designated as mainly teaching, mainly research or mainly community service. All of an individual's projects could be presented together to indicate the full scope of work undertaken. Cross-referencing between different projects and different areas of academic work was to be encouraged.

The initial work of Eric and Maria drew heavily on existing work on portfolio development (see, for example, Ramsden *et al.* 1995). This work, however, focuses on the presenting of information rather than on the initial collecting, exploring and documenting of that information. Eric and Maria wanted to emphasize the latter. They suggested that information be documented around the following headings:

- Title and type of project (e.g. teaching /research/community service).
- Philosophy: what basic principles underpin the project and why.
- Reading/learning: what has been most influential in what you have read and studied and learned.
- Who are the students or clients.
- The context: classroom, studio, laboratory, workplace.
- Aims and objectives.
- Anticipated outcomes.
- Practice: what have you done and what you have learned.
- Evaluation: who has evaluated what and how.
- Personal learning: what has been learned and how has/will practice change.
- Communication as a result of learning: what has been formally communicated – meetings, conferences, papers and so forth.

After developing the above guidelines, Eric and Maria set about testing them. Both tried to use them to document the development of the new curriculum and Maria also tried to use it to record her work on developing disability projects with the industry consortium. They found the task both complex and time-consuming. They had difficulty using the headings they had constructed and when they tried to devise others, they made the task even more complex. Before the end of first semester, they agreed that their guidelines were unrealistic.

Through ongoing discussion with Ted (the head of department), the following points emerged:

- It is difficult to devise a system which simultaneously documents activity and presents it in a portfolio form.
- Each project should be established with a description which broadly responds to the first five questions on the original list, that is, philosophy, background, context and intended aims and objectives and outcomes.

- The ongoing process should be loosely documented in terms of actions, results and reflections.
- The evaluation should be documented in terms of what feedback was being sought, from whom, in what form – and reflections.
- A final report (between one and two pages) should summarize the project, its achievements, the problems encountered and what was learned and what will be changed. Also what has been communicated through talks, papers or publications.

The university's Committee on Promotion Review made significant use of the work of Eric and Maria in developing the new university policy on academic promotion. The new guidelines insisted on separate teaching and community service portfolios. A research portfolio remained an option. Candidates could still submit research evidence in the conventional form of lists of publications, grants and so forth. The structure of all portfolios was to be as follows:

- Background: personal history and institutional context.
- Philosophy: what informs your work and what are the implications for practice.
- Selected evidence: a minimum of three projects, described under the following headings.
  Issue/problem
  Background
  Context
  Aims and objectives
  Methods
  Outcomes
  Evaluation
  Broader relevance and discussion

Case study conclusion

Maria received her promotion the following year. Eric was not successful, but intends to try again. He has now worked through three student/industry projects with a firm of bicycle manufacturers and is exhilarated by the news that the design of one of his students has been bought by a Swedish company for manufacture in Europe.

The department itself is doing well; it now has eight research students working on projects devised through the consortium developed by Ted and Simon. The undergraduate course has been revamped and includes design tasks which work on real problems from the third week in first year. Students are more positive about their learning experiences and the morale of both the students and the staff is high. The department is one of the few departments within the university where there is willing and ongoing documentation of academic work and Ted has spoken both internally to senior leaders and, nationally, at conferences about how this has been achieved.

Reflections

When Ted speaks formally about his success in getting accountability mechanisms embedded into his department, he uses six overheads. Each of these overheads represents what he believes to be an essential piece of advice:

- Work with academic staff – build on and work with their ideas.
- Help staff to see all the changes as working together towards a single desirable end.
- If it's worthwhile, it's worthwhile documenting.
- Give staff the freedom to devise their own systems.
- Give staff guidance and support and feedback in order that they end up with something that works.
- Ensure that what is documented is supported by the staff and rewarded by the university.

This advice is worthwhile and neatly reflects the issues raised at the beginning of this chapter.

This chapter began by drawing parallels between assessment and accountability and we will conclude in a similar fashion. It has been argued that accountability, like assessment, can be a potent force both for and against learning. In the best cases, it can give crucial messages concerning what is valued by the organization and it can both guide and support staff to engage with major issues and problems. There was plenty of evidence of this in the case study. Too often, however, the push for accountability gives inconsistent messages concerning what is valued by the university and it encourages staff to adopt minimalist strategies towards their work in order to satisfy the surface demands of the accountability systems.

For instance, in one university with which the author is familiar, there is a monolithic quality system in place. The university has laboured hard to win the commitment of the staff, but has not succeeded. Consequently, it has resorted to insisting on compliance and the staff who do not comply are penalized. For example, a necessary condition of taking leave is that all the administrative tasks, including documentation for accountability purposes, is up to date. At one level, this ploy works and the administration and documentation is done – albeit, minimally. The university believes it has won, but it has only won minimalist attention to a bureaucratic system. It has not even begun to address the improvement or maintenance of the quality of academic work which is, of course, what such systems are supposed to be about.

One of the authors' favourite comments on teaching comes from W.W. Sawyer, a teacher and writer on mathematics. Sawyer states:

> Nearly every subject has a shadow or imitation. It would, I suppose, be quite possible to teach a deaf and dumb child to play the piano. When it played a wrong note, it would see the frown of its teacher and try again. But it would obviously have no idea of what it was doing or why

> anyone would devote hours to such an extraordinary exercise. It would have learnt an imitation of music. And it would have learnt to fear the piano exactly as most students fear what is supposed to be mathematics.
>
> (Quoted in Ramsden 1992: 38)

Sawyer goes on to say that what is true for mathematics is equally true for other subjects. It seems clear that it is also true for quality-assurance systems. If quality-assurance systems are to be more than elaborate shams to hide falling morale and questionable practice, then universities must encourage staff to see the essential purpose behind these systems and, as a consequence, to become committed rather than compliant – and universities must provide both the support and guidance to achieve this outcome.

This chapter, however, has not been just about quality assurance (or accountability); it has been about the balance between accountability and reward and it has been argued that salient documentation is the link. Salient documentation provides a resource for reflection and learning in staff and it provides evidence of action and change which supports the university accountability mechanisms and the records of development and achievement of individual staff. The documentation, so much criticized by the academic staff in the interviews in Chapter 2, has another side. It is a liberating side well worth exploring. If we, as academic staff, are willing and able to learn in the face of university changes and if we want that learning to be recognized and rewarded and to benefit others, then we must be willing to make a record of our learning and changed practice and recognize that such recording and communicating with colleagues is at the heart of scholarly practice. Many times over the years, the author has asserted the idea expressed so eloquently below by A.N. Whitehead, that the value of teaching is not in writing about it, but in its act:

> Mankind is as individual in its mode of output as in the substance of its thoughts. For some of the most fertile minds composition in writing, or in a form reducible to writing, seems to be an impossibility. In every faculty you will find that some of the more brilliant teachers are not among those who publish. Their originality requires for its expression direct intercourse with their pupils in the form of personal discussion. Such men exercise an immense influence; and yet, after the generation of their pupils has passed away, they sleep among the innumerable unthanked benefactors of humanity. Fortunately, one of them is immortal – Socrates.
>
> (Whitehead 1967: 148–9)

Let us not forget that the reason we know of Socrates is because there was a skilled scribe called Plato on hand. As teachers, we must be our own Plato. We must document our own discoveries and achievements and hopefully we, and others, will learn and profit from reflection on this documentation.

9

Encouraging Change: Valuing the Past, Preparing for the Future

> Habit is not to be flung out of the window by any man, but coaxed downstairs a step at a time.
>
> (Mark Twain)

Introduction

When we are told to change our way of working, we are likely to feel threatened. Our sense of professionalism and our sense of worth both take a tumble. Most of us need help to give up on aspects of our work which we value but which are no longer seen as appropriate. We need help to move on to something which looks uncertain and alien, and we need assistance which is informed, planned, consistent and concerted. Table 9.1 summarizes those feelings as expressed by academic staff. It also summarized salient advice in the literature. A significant proportion of academic staff in our universities need help. Those in leadership positions are sometimes able to point to initiatives taken in this direction. They have organized a workshop or two to discuss the issues or to develop appropriate skills, or they might even have offered grants or other incentives to get new practices under way. Such initiatives are laudable but they will have limited impact if they are occasional or one-off events. There is an enormous task to be undertaken and concerted effort is necessary.

When ICI North America moved towards a new way of working, it invested over a billion dollars into supporting and developing the staff in its leading plants and agencies (Senge 1992). Ford Australia has spent over $6 million in the last five years in retraining and supporting staff to match the company's change in vision and direction (*The Australian*, 6 May 1996). It is not argued that similar resources be dedicated to support change in higher education, but there is a need for some committed, concerted and informed support. Without this, universities, academic staff and the public they serve, will suffer. William Bridges (1991) in *Managing Transitions*, puts it thus:

Table 9.1 Encouraging change

Area of concern			
Academic staff in non-leadership roles say:	*Academic staff in leadership roles say:*	*Student learning literature says:*	*Learning organization literature says:*
'People are not valued. Their past and present achievements are ignored.'	'Leaders also feel undervalued and undersupported.' 'Staff complain too much. Change agendas have to be attended to otherwise departments and/or units will close, jobs will go.'	'Regular and supportive feedback is necessary for learning. Learning involves change.'	'Change can be painful but also liberating.' 'Support, including the opportunity for new learning and for personal development, is essential.'

> The single biggest reason organizational changes fail is that no-one thought about endings or planned to manage their impact on people. Naturally concerned about the future, planners and implementers usually forget the people have to let go of the present first. They forget that while the first task of change management is to understand the destination and how to get there the first task of transition management is to convince people to leave home. You'll save yourself a lot of grief if you remember that.
>
> (Bridges 1991: 32)

Bridges models the process of change as three stages. The first is helping staff to let go of the past and the present. The second is helping staff to move through a time of transition when all is uncertain and the future is far from clear. The third is the new beginning when tentative steps forward are being taken, but uncertainty is still the dominant emotion. In this chapter, we look at helping staff to change in terms of these three stages and use the case study of two amalgamating departments as illustration.

Stage one: Letting go of the past

Treat the past with respect

We spend a good many hours of our day and week involved in our academic work and in reflection on this work. It is hardly surprising, then, that our identity is tied up with this work and that when we are pushed to change, there is some resistance. At times of change, we are likely to be more emotional than rational, more defensive than creative. We are likely to need support to move successfully through the change.

Change does not have to involve either criticism of the past or of existing practice. The practice of the past and the present will almost always have aspects of excellence. In preparing for a different future, we are better able to cope if the good things are built upon. This does *not* mean making superficial changes. It means taking aspects of good practice and fundamental principles which are relevant in the face of changed circumstances and reinterpreting them. It is easy for those already sold on the need to change to focus on the future and to undervalue what has gone before, but undervaluing what is still precious to some of our colleagues will not, in the long run, help to achieve successful transitions. It takes time for us to grow into changes and we will do it easier and more successfully if we are supported and help others to build on what has gone before. The case study explored in this chapter offers an excellent example of this. The merging departments of sociology and leisure and tourism, in a university established in the 1970s, had numerous bad-tempered meetings between staff at all levels during a one-month period. The espoused aim of the meetings was to plan different aspects of their joint future, particularly the development of a new undergraduate course. The discussions which ensued had, more often than not, served to expose and to deepen feelings of bitterness and resentment between the two cohorts of staff. In a meeting between the two heads of department and the dean, the head of sociology commented that the sociology department was 25-years-old to the day. The department had been one of the first to be established when the university was founded. The present head had been a student in the department's first intake of students.

The dean mentioned this to the deputy vice-chancellor (DVC) and he agreed that the merger plans be pushed to the background for a time, while the department organize a series of events to mark the achievements and highlights of the department over the past 25 years. It became clear that the department did have a good deal to celebrate. It had several famous graduates as well as staff who had contributed to significant pieces of research and policy work and who had authored major books in the field. But, perhaps most importantly within the context of the merger, it had been the first such department in the country to have had a work-based learning component. This component had been developed for students in the early 1980s and had taken up one teaching term. Students had worked in a range of government and private sector organizations in order to observe, map and comment upon the social structures and interactions within the organizations. On numerous occasions, the work of the students had informed subsequent reorganizations or had contributed to more thorough reviews. The scheme had fallen by the wayside as student numbers had grown and it had become increasingly difficult to find placements. But it was this scheme, in particular, which impressed the staff of the leisure and tourism department whose own work-placement scheme was at a low ebb. The celebrations had the effect of raising the morale in the sociology department and of making public the many achievements of a department which was sometimes seen by others, particularly those in the leisure and tourism department, to be 'arrogant' and 'old-fashioned'.

The leisure and tourism department, by contrast, was just five years old. It was agreed that this department should also have an event to celebrate its five years in the university and its story was a very different one. It was one of rapid growth, challenges with a new type of university student and challenges with immigrant and international students. Former students came along and paid their respects and spoke of their gratitude. There could be no doubt that over the past five years, the department had had some remarkable achievements.

These acts of celebration did much to assist the merger. Although the celebrations dominated for a couple of months, the pace of the merger plans increased rather than decreased. In particular, the work-based learning component of the old sociology course was warmly acclaimed and accepted as the basis for work-based learning in the new joint undergraduate course. It was seen as particularly useful that students work on a specific, negotiated project, and that progress be reviewed monthly at a meeting attended by a work supervisor, a university supervisor and the student.

Overall, the celebrations made all the staff proud of their own past, respectful of the past of others, more aware of the others' sense of loss and attuned to their history and ambitions. From a very shaky start, the celebrations set the merger on its feet again though, as we shall soon see, there were many ups and downs still to come.

Expect overreaction

It takes a long time to come to terms with change and with the loss which change implies. This simple fact *cannot* be overemphasized. It is likely to be several weeks after the major announcements when despair or anger or resentment hits most strongly. By this time, it is often assumed that the staff will have accepted the idea of change and that they should be thinking ahead to the future. Outbursts of distress or anger at this time are, consequently, unexpected and appear to be unreasonable. For some staff, however, the real consequences are only just becoming apparent and a strong reaction is likely.

In the case study, the announcement that the merger would go ahead had been made on a Monday morning by the dean at a special meeting. A letter explaining the merger and stressing that there would be no compulsory redundancies went out on the same day. The announcement had been expected by the staff for some time. The heads had discussed it with their groups and had indicated that the merger was a possibility some two or three months previously. The university was rationalizing its departments and, in some cases, its faculties. Smaller groups were being joined together with larger groups. The question, it seemed to most staff, was not if they would be merged, but with whom they would merge and when. Staff of the sociology department had assumed a merger with social work to be the most likely, and the most acceptable, outcome. The department of leisure and tourism, on the other hand, owing to their growing student numbers, had hoped that they might escape merger with any other group.

For a week there was subdued, but seemingly reasonable, debate and discussion of the issue within the two departments. The heads almost began to believe that things would go smoother than they had dared hope. But at a staff meeting about a fortnight after the formal announcement, there was a vicious verbal attack on the head of sociology by one of his staff and this attack was supported and sustained by other members of staff, a couple of whom were usually strong supporters of the head. The head was alarmed and surprised to hear these staff members not just being critical, but being vindictive. At the centre of the criticism was an allegation that the head had negotiated this merger with leisure and tourism to save his own job. The head's academic record gave him a distinct advantage over the head of leisure and tourism in a competition for the new head of department position. In a similar competition with the head of social work, he would not have had such a clear advantage.

Distressed at the outbursts, the head closed the meeting without addressing this central accusation. He went to his office but was followed by the main protagonist who forced his way into the head's office and restated his complaints and a range of other grievances even more loudly and aggressively than had been done during the general meeting. The two staff members who had supported the protagonist during the open meeting disapproved of this action and later met with the head to express condemnation of their colleague's behaviour, but also to reinforce the perception there was much anger and resentment in the department and that the head should attend to it.

A couple of days later, over a coffee break, the main protagonist accused both of these staff members of having been 'bribed' into supporting the head and a series of unpleasant exchanges between several members of staff took place.

The head, at the next staff meeting, restated the reasons why the dean and the DVC had decided on the merger with leisure and tourism and added some additional information as to why the merger with social work had not been seen as appropriate. He explained that the management structure of the new combined department had not yet been decided upon. It had, however, been discussed and he had let it be known that he was not desirous of keeping his head of department status; it was a responsibility which he believed that he had carried long enough. He concluded that he understood that all members of the department were distressed at the thought of the loss and that it was reasonable to be sad, and perhaps even resentful, when something as fine as their old department was being forced to come to an end. He emphasized, however, that neither he, nor any other members of staff, were the catalyst for the changes.

The head believed that this talk had helped considerably to calm people down. He was wrong. There was still anger and concern. He talked of cancelling the staff meeting the following week because he felt that he had done all that he could. But loyal members of the department urged him to continue in his role of listening and being sympathetic, at least for a little while yet. He did so for two more staff meetings and numerous individual meetings. At last, it seemed that the anger began to subside.

The head observed later that this period had probably been the most difficult of the merger. He had felt powerless. On the one hand, he was being pushed by the dean to stop the nonsense and to take control and, on the other hand, he was being encouraged by loyal members of his staff to ride the storm and to give people time. He stressed that it was very important to tell himself that the resentment and anger were not really directed towards him, but rather at what had happened and that people who are experiencing loss are likely to behave irrationally. He also went on to state how important it was to have staff express their loyalty and support. The head was particularly keen to acknowledge that things got better not just because he did certain things – things got better because the group were able to support each other.

It is interesting to note that six months later, at another staff meeting, the protagonist who had initially been so angry and abusive, actually criticized his colleagues for dragging their feet with the merger!

Share information

Making allowances for anger and insisting that it takes time for people to change is not an excuse for inaction. The main activity during these early days has to be the providing and the sharing of information. There are numerous reasons why information is not shared at times of change and some of them are more noble than others. Among the more well-meaning are:

- 'It will only upset people and all is not resolved yet.' It is important to know, however, that the grapevine will almost certainly have hint of the change and will likely elaborate and thus do far more damage than a factual announcement ever would.
- 'People already know, it was announced at a meeting or in some form of communication last week.' People may have been told, but they may not have really heard. Information which is threatening is often accepted very slowly. There is often an assumption that the change 'won't really affect me'. It is a good idea, therefore, to give the information continually in many different ways, so that it becomes clear that it *will* affect people and to clarify just what the effect will be.

Naturally, we all will find occasions when we believe that particular information is best withheld, but we must act with caution. The cost of withholding may well be more than the cost of revealing. Most of the time, we withhold information because we fear the consequences of revealing it. We fear the emotion likely to be generated – but the short-term emotion is likely to be less damaging both to individuals and to the organization than the long-term resentment generated when it is found that information has been withheld.

This case study provides several examples of information giving and concealing and the consequences of both forms of action.

The dean had wanted to wait until after the Easter break to make the announcement concerning the merger. Both the heads of the merging departments had advised an immediate announcement and warned that word would get out. It always did and to begin from a situation where the truth was being concealed was not a good start.

Following the first announcement, the dean held no more open information sessions for the staff involved in the merger. The dean argued that the announcement had been made; the letter clarifying the situation had been distributed and that was all that needed to be done.

The heads, on the other hand, believed there was a need to provide more information. There were many concerns about both professionalism and the future of subjects and courses within the departments. At the back of the minds of most staff was a concern about redundancy. But there was also another dominant fear which is often overlooked. The staff feared loss of status. Academic status is the most salient currency in a university and the staff, like so many during times of change, feared being marginalized and having their reputations devalued. This underlying fear was hidden behind the expressed concern by the staff from sociology as a concern about standards, academic rigour and discipline-based knowledge. In the new combined department, the staff from sociology feared that their experience and reputation as scholars would be sacrificed to a shallow, but highly commercial, vocationalism.

Both heads held numerous meetings: some with individual staff members; some with small groups of staff; and some with all the staff. The heads attempted to put minds at rest and insist that a new, joint way forward could be found which did not sacrifice standards but did respond to new demands. It was a challenging task! Not only was it very time-consuming, but some of the staff were convinced that the lack of information from the dean meant that the information which they were being given was deliberately not accurate. Both of the heads appealed to the dean to attend a joint staff meeting of both departments and to endorse the information given so far and to answer questions. In the final event, this meeting was also attended by the DVC who had heard of the concerns and had a special interest in the merger because of his discipline background in the social sciences.

Both the dean and the DVC answered questions openly and, in response to one question, the DVC became particularly expansive about the nature and future of the new department. He emphasized the qualities and strengths of both groups and how the combination could be a formidable partnership making the new department the best in the country, possibly the world. He insisted that the university wanted a new department with academic status as well as professional respectability. He emphasized that how the new department developed was largely the responsibility of the staff and it was an amazing opportunity for all of them. Because of his discipline background, the DVC promised that he would take a particular interest in how things developed.

Probably nothing substantive was said at this meeting that had not been said before, but the tone of openness and optimism set by the DVC meant that the meeting ended on a high note with the staff feeling more reassured than previously and more at ease.

What has just been described illustrates a common response of those in leadership positions; they tend to make a major announcement and then pass on additional or emerging information through supervisors. Below, another situation is described where problems arose because the important task of further communication was delegated. Above, it has been argued that the message is not necessarily believed unless it comes from the top. Below we indicate how the message is sometimes misrepresented when it passes through several hands.

Misrepresented information

For about two weeks, the head of leisure and tourism had meetings with only the subject coordinators. He worked on the assumption that they would act as the source of information for the academic staff within their groups. But the strategy had some very unhelpful consequences. One of the coordinators felt particularly threatened by the merger and essentially played power games with her colleagues; she selectively gave and hid information. The resulting conspiracies and accusations within the department took the head a good deal of time to resolve and served as a sound lesson of what not to do. The head stated that he learned two things as a result of this failed strategy. First, that information is power and must be shared equally. Secondly, that when some people feel threatened, they are likely to seek power and use it to their own advantage.

Be aware of the threat of loss of position and loss of status

It has been proposed above that status and reputation are the most salient currency of academic staff. For better or worse, most people are more likely to see a change positively if they believe that it will not challenge their existing status or, better still, that it will offer an opportunity for increased development and enhanced status.

In the present case study, the academic staff expected friction over who was to be the new head of the combined department. But they were much less prepared for the subtle power-plays for position and status among the more junior members of the merging departments.

As seen above, the head of sociology was keen to relinquish his head of department status and to return to a stronger research focus. He had a personal chair in the university and saw the opportunities available in developing the research profile of the new combined department.

Those who felt most threatened were the coordinators of the courses and of the subjects. It was clear that new courses and subjects would have to be developed, but who would head these was not obvious. Initially, it was the coordinators in leisure and tourism who felt most concerned. As highlighted earlier, one of these coordinators used the information she had received from the head in order to manipulate her colleagues for her own ends. Sometimes, she deliberately stretched the truth and sometimes she withheld the truth, but overall her aim was to maintain her position as a course leader against any possible threat from the staff in sociology. In the leisure and tourism department, teaching responsibility had a high status because the vocationally-attractive courses which were offered had been a major factor in the rapid growth of the department.

In sociology, on the other hand, the task of coordinating or leading a subject or course was usually not seen to be such a high-status task. Status, on the whole, was associated with research and, therefore, coordination responsibilities left little time to maintain research productivity. Once it became obvious that there was something to fight over, however, the existing coordinators in sociology became much more protective of their responsibilities. They started expressing a commitment to course and subject design and planning which they had never before expressed so strongly.

The head of sociology made it known to his staff that he was not applying for the new head's position. He viewed the opportunity to return to his research as a welcome one. He eventually spoke enthusiastically of plans for developing the new combined department's research profile and asked for expressions of interest in developing, coordinating and leading postgraduate programs. This was a welcome opportunity for a couple of undergraduate coordinators from sociology who now happily refocused their ambitions. Thus, it was not long before the coordinators in both departments ceased to feel threatened by the issue of who might do what. Each settled back believing that in the new department their status and value would be maintained whether they were coordinating courses or subjects at the undergraduate or postgraduate level.

Stage two: Moving through the transition

It has been pointed out that time must be given to endings and that endings should not be rushed. Equally, of course, it must be acknowledged that they should not be allowed to go on for too long. There is a fine balance to be struck between hurrying and prolonging change. In the instance of the present case study, where a major amalgamation was happening, it took three months before all the staff were able to move on into the transition period; this is the period when they were able to take tentative, but genuine, steps towards establishing a new role and identity.

In many ways, this transition period is the bleakest time of the change. Staff remain uncertain about what the future holds, but they know that they have lost the past. It is the time when senior people often expect things to happen and bright new plans to emerge, but this is precisely the time when many staff feel particularly dislocated and lost and incapable of either planning or being proactive.

The following headings pick up on advice offered in the literature on finding a successful way through this difficult period. Bridges (1991) and Pascale (1990) have been drawn on in particular. These headings also reflect aspects of good practice identified in the case study.

See the change as an opportunity

When systems and jobs are working well, it is extremely difficult to contemplate change. Why change things when they are, on the whole, working well? Once change is inevitable, however, it becomes easier to see opportunities.

The head of leisure and tourism suggested a day's workshop to focus on the opportunities and challenges which the merger would bring. Much of the morning was taken up by a facilitator who lead the staff of both departments through an exercise in creative thinking, using the context of their own merger as a starting-point. The intention was to ensure that creative as well as common-sense responses got an airing. By the end of the workshop, a number of ideas and directions were endorsed by both departments as having potential. The ideas and directions were then presented to the dean and the DVC who attended for this part of the workshop. The DVC then commented on what was presented in the light of the strategic directions of the university, supporting some ideas and possible directions and advising caution with others.

Training and development, as required

It is often difficult to know how to prepare for change. It is clear that new skills and new ways of working are likely to be needed but just what they will be and when is the best time to develop them is not so clear.

Returning to the case study, early in the amalgamation, it was agreed by the heads that a number of developmental workshops would be helpful. The workshop on creative thinking was commented on earlier. Another, on team work, and a third on flexible teaching, were also planned and provided.

Initially, the workshops on team work and on flexible teaching were not successful. The one on team work floundered because no-one really knew who would be in the new teams or what the purpose or focus of the teams would be. The third on flexible teaching failed because at this stage there was still much resistance to the idea of students and teachers working in anything other than a face-to-face teaching and learning situation.

Both of these workshops were held again about six months later with considerably more success. By this time, directions were more firmly established, flexible teaching appeared a less threatening alternative, and the staff themselves were requesting guidance in these areas.

Rationalize the changes

At one level, it can be argued that academic life is one of non-stop change and there is some truth in this, but some changes are bigger than others and it is important when confronted with a major change not to get side-tracked with changes which are incidental and unrelated. This will have a disruptive effect. Changes can often nest one inside the other, and the development and planning of a smaller component before the larger one has been planned or addressed is often of limited use.

In the case study, the university was introducing new accountability measures for the evaluation of students. Each faculty was to put forward a faculty plan and details of how this would work in each of its departments. The deadline for the faculty document, including what this would look like in the new combined department of sociology and leisure and tourism was due some three months after the announcement of the amalgamation. There was little hope that a bona fide response, which was in line with the directions of the new department, would be developed in time. The dean, nevertheless, expected that it be done. The heads insisted that this would be a futile exercise at the current stage and said that the response would be done during the course of the replanning. It was also pointed out that to place additional pressure on the staff would likely have negative effects on their morale and the ultimate success of the new department. The heads consulted and decided to jointly stand against the dean. They sent a letter formally explaining their position to the dean with a copy to the DVC. Both heads were reprimanded by the dean and there was no formal response from the DVC but, in the end, they got their way and the staff of the newly-merged department remained protected from that particular demand until later in their planning.

Time release to devise, develop and plan changes

A major change creates an enormous amount of extra work. Academic staff already work long hours and to be required to take on a major additional load can lead to feelings of resentment, frustration and high anxiety. The staff may well want to be involved in shaping the changes but find that existing workloads leave them little time or energy to do so and little ability to be creative in their approach. Sometimes what happens is that a consultant is called in to work on the replanning. Strategies emerge, but they are not owned by the staff affected by the major change. In the case study of this chapter, an alternative response was made.

The dean had originally agreed that a sum of money be set aside for the hiring of a consultant to help carry out the replanning. The two heads persuaded him that it was a better idea to release their own staff to do this and to hire casual teaching staff and tutors instead. This was agreed upon. Two staff members, one from each department, were released from a large part of their teaching load. Two other staff members had some time release and some of the other staff were supported with help in marking. As a result, each week, a half-day was set aside as a planning afternoon. The half-day started with a lunch-time update of the progress which had already been achieved and the afternoon then proceeded with the meeting of a range of working parties and committees. The result was a planning process which almost all of the staff felt a part of.

Develop a purpose, a picture, a plan and a part to play for all staff

Before a plan can be developed, those involved must be clear about what the achievable outcomes might look like, what the change is about and why it is necessary. Often a plan only outlines the large-scale changes, for instance, when certain documents will be ready, when students will be admitted and so forth. However, the more detailed planning of steps and schedules for individuals and smaller groups also needs attention and, most importantly, the part that each individual member of the group will play. Bridges (1991: 55–9) emphasizes the importance of staff having a purpose, a picture, a plan and part to play. Let us consider how this applies to the case study.

Purpose

It is contended that when people are unconvinced that change has to happen then they are unlikely to put themselves behind the change (Fullan 1994). First of all, they need to be convinced that there is a problem and have a clear understanding of the nature of the problem. The next step is to think through what may, or may not happen, if the problem is not addressed and, most importantly, what will happen to them and their colleagues if the problem is ignored.

In this case study, it was repeatedly emphasized to the staff by the head, by the dean and by the DVC that there was a need to rationalize units within the university in order to create larger units and so economize on the administration. There was also a need to create distinctive courses which would attract students both locally and overseas. The staff were able to see that the merger would address both of these concerns.

A picture

Ideas about purpose are essential but, by themselves, they are not enough. Some people find it helpful to change if they can see what the change might look like and if they can explore how the purpose will develop through a series of pictures of themselves and their associates working in the new situation. Almost certainly, the picture will not accurately reflect the way things happen, but the aim is not this – the aim is to give an indication of the way things might be and to act as a support and a guide.

In the case study, the pictures conjured up by the staff in the different groups were very different. Staff in sociology worked with pictures which ranged from images of students deconstructing aspects of popular culture, to the development of research studies on conceptions of 'work' and 'leisure' in different social groups. Staff in leisure and tourism worked, for instance, with pictures of students undertaking projects which explored the social expectations of a range of different tourist groups. The images were different, but members of each group found it possible to generate them and to work together to further generate and refine them.

A plan

Having a picture helps to expand and explore the purpose, but it does *not* help to move things forward. A plan, and probably more than one plan, is necessary for this. Change, certainly any major change, will involve at least two different sorts of planning. The first sort is the sort we are most familiar with. It means fitting what has to be done into the timeframe available. We work backwards, starting from the time the change has to happen on formal timetables and we accordingly compress or expand the time available. For instance, for a course to be up and running by September, it has to be through council by a certain date, and through academic board by another date and so on. But there is another sort of planning to be done and this is the planning that is often neglected. It also works in the opposite way.

This other sort of planning involves helping people to change and this means working *forwards* from where we are rather than working backwards from where we want to be. These plans involve taking into account what has to be done to help the group to change and also involve giving time for the group to recover from the loss experienced when valued aspects of work cease. Time needs to be allocated to developing new ways of looking at, and understanding, the changing environment and in re-enthusing, reskilling and retraining.

Occasionally, of course, the two sorts of plans, the preparation of the people and the formal timetabling, will come together but, typically, they do not. Certainly, they did not in this case study. The dean was constantly pushing to move because he was close to the structural processes of the formal timetable. The heads held back somewhat because they knew the unprepared state of many of the staff. It is important for those working with change to realize that structural plans and timetables and personal change are very different. The head of Sociology, in a response to the dean, wrote a memo of which the following is an extract:

> Certainly, I can produce a combined staff list, but this does not mean that staff think and act as a single department . . . I can pass over the draft course outline for consideration by courses committee, but this does not mean that teachers have come to terms with what it is students will learn and how they will come to know this . . . We both want the same outcome but at this stage we have different concerns.

The concern of the head was to help the staff to make a new beginning and not to allow university procedures to get in the way of this. The concern of the dean was to ensure that the due processes were attended to at the right time. Thus, it was inevitable that there would be tension. It is good there was, for it meant that in this change situation the needs of the departmental people were being addressed and it also meant, that in the end, the change was a successful and useful experience rather than a bitter and debilitating one.

A part to play

Perhaps, above all, we need to feel that in the new scheme of things there is a role; a part for us to play – not just a desk and chair, but a specific contribution which is expected and which we are challenged to make. Until we are helped to see and understand the particular contribution we can make and, until this particular contribution is generally acknowledged, it is likely we will spend more time looking around for alternative opportunities than focusing on making the group work and addressing the part we can play in making it work.

In the merging departments of the case study, the two departmental administrators were most concerned about their new roles and responsibilities. Both were women in their thirties with some ambition. They were both graduates and both were looking for opportunities for development. The administrator of leisure and tourism had a business degree and the administrator in sociology was, like the head, a former graduate of the department. She had done casual work in the department after graduating. She had stepped into the administrator's job on a temporary basis but four years later was made permanent. She got on very well with the students and, on more than one occasion, had eased trouble between student representatives and the department. Some years previously, she had considered doing a Master's qualification in industrial relations but had never done anything about it. The administrator from leisure and tourism was very competent at handling the financial side of the department and in this department, with increasing numbers of full-fee-paying students, this was a noted advantage.

The heads explained to the administrators that both would maintain their present salary and level of appointment but that they must come to an agreement on the division of work and responsibilities acceptable to themselves, the heads and the dean. It was acknowledged that their strengths and interests represented different aspects of work and that a division which built on these strengths would be welcomed.

It was not too difficult for the administrator for leisure and tourism to take overall budget responsibilities and to feel happy about this. In this university, as in most, status in the administrative ranks was gained by handling finances. If budgetary dealings were a significant part of the task then the level of appointment was higher than if the burden of the task was handling people. (This, in itself, is a telling comment on the priorities of universities.) Consequently, taking budgetary responsibilities away from the sociology administrator and making her responsible for personnel and student administration might have suited her, but might be seen by others as a demotion. There had to be something extra within the new role for it to be seen as a more equal sharing of responsibility and status.

In the new combined department, there would be almost 600 students, including full-fee-paying students and students involved in the flexible delivery. The students' union had, for some time, been concerned about the inadequate attention the university gave to day-to-day dealings with students outside of the teaching responsibilities. Every year, the inefficiency of administrative procedures were a major concern. For some time, the union had pushed for better procedures and for a quality assurance system to be introduced. The sociology administrator was aware of this and agreed to take on overall responsibility for all student-related matters, so long as the new department would develop and trial quality assurance measures similar to those advocated by the students' union. This was agreed upon, and this would be the administrator's particular responsibility. This would be a university first. It attracted comment and interest from the students' union and from senior management within the university.

In the end, both administrators were happy that they had a significant part to play in the new department.

Stage three: New beginnings

The point made above, that the formal diary of events does not represent where people are, is particularly relevant when we talk about beginnings. Craig Hickman (1992) talks about beginnings being a psychological phenomenon, not an organizational one. He distinguishes between 'starts', which represent the organizational life and which can be planned and 'beginnings' which represent personal experiences and have to be nurtured. This is a salient idea to keep in mind during changes and innovations. 'Something' can have started according to a timetable but we as the people involved may not yet be ready to begin. Even where there has been a commitment by us during the intermediate planning stage, we are likely to demonstrate anxiety as the time for the formal 'start' comes close. We know there is a possibility that the new endeavour may not work and yet now there is no turning back. It is important to expect some degree of hesitation in ourselves and in others.

In the case study, the member of staff from the old sociology department who had initially been the most antagonistic, but who had lately become one of the most committed, suddenly began to be less positive once the new year began and he was the coordinator for a subject in the new combined department. He had over a hundred students doing his first-year subject and he had planned it thoroughly and carefully, but for the first few weeks he was far from positive. He criticized the students, the new department, the tutors, the materials and so forth.

The former head of leisure and tourism, who was now acting as head of the new combined department, called him into his office for a chat. The intention had been to find out what was troubling the staff member. The outcome was far from happy. The staff member felt under attack and, worse still, under attack by a stranger whom he believed knew nothing about the subject or the situation.

Advice was sought from the former head of sociology, who was now acting as a sub-dean within the faculty, with a responsibility for developing research. The former head of sociology called into the staffroom when he knew that the staff member would be there. The new sub-dean made a number of positive comments about what he had heard about the new subject: that it was innovative in content and teaching methods; that it was challenging for students, but that it must also be a great challenge to teach; and that he admired the staff member for developing and taking on the subject.

Several times over the following weeks, the staff member sought out the advice of his former head over issues relating to the new subject and over these weeks he became noticeably more confident and positive. The staff member later confided to his former head that the positive feedback had indeed come at a crucial time. He had been feeling overburdened and uncertain and was looking longingly back to the good old days when they had taught together a traditional first-year sociology course.

Celebrate successes as soon as possible

The more far-reaching a change, the longer it will take for new advantages to be realized and, consequently, the more important it is to create intermediate goals and opportunities for success and celebration along the way. Without such opportunities, those who still have doubts can readily turn into critics and spread discontent. Short-term successes help reinforce the belief that the changes are working and that even bigger and more salient successes are around the corner.

In this case study, there was a celebratory cheese and wine reception attended by the dean and DVC of the evening of the first official day of the new combined department. Such a celebration was symbolically important because it underlined that the change had, at least structurally, taken place and there was now a new formal identity. But during the first months of the amalgamation, a number of other achievements were also highlighted and publicly acknowledged.

The new undergraduate degree course was cited by a professional association as an example of good practice. This was acknowledged at a faculty board meeting as well as at a departmental meeting and a bottle of champagne was opened one Friday afternoon. There was negligible student dropout from the course during the first three months and the formal student feedback collected at the conclusion of the first couple of topics was, overall, very favourable. This was a considerable improvement on the old undergraduate courses in the former departments of sociology and leisure and tourism. In both cases, drop-out rates had been around 25 per cent and, amongst those who stayed, there had been a small but vocal group of discontented students critical of both the teaching methods and the course content. The good news was given by the course coordinator at a departmental staff meeting and later commented upon at a meeting of faculty board. There was also strong interest being shown in the course by a Japanese university. All these events were seen to justify the opening of another bottle of champagne on another Friday night a little later in the year.

Conclusion

This chapter has been about attending to endings as well as beginnings. The story of the merger between the departments of sociology and leisure and tourism has illustrated some of the advice which comes out of the literature on coping with change, particularly Bridges (1991) and Pascale (1990). The unhappy comments of staff, cited in Chapter 2, emphasize how seriously this advice should be taken. Central to this advice is the idea that we, as staff, have to be supported and to support others to mourn endings before taking on new beginnings and that there needs to be a period of transition when we work through our loss and establish new directions.

The trouble is, of course, that universities face so many changes and so many endings and beginnings that it might be argued that the important thing is to help staff to cope with constant change. What is usually meant by constant change is, in fact, no more an *increased rate* of change. It certainly does *not* mean changing everything continually. More pressure for change, as we saw earlier in the chapter, means more attention to priorities, more attention to weighing external directions and internal capacities and prioritizing some areas for attention while holding others stable. It means heeding the overall purpose of our work within the university and sometimes being ready to sacrifice processes and objectives in favour of new directions. There will undoubtedly be losses just as there will undoubtedly be creative opportunities.

At one level, we have human nature on our side. It has, over time, a remarkable capacity to adapt to the constant rate of change. Put our grandparents into the situations we now face daily and they would not cope. And indeed, put us back into the times of our grandparents and we would almost certainly become frustrated by the lack of change. Having said this, however, there is another side of human nature which must be attended to and that is our need to hold on to aspects of our past experience. We feel comfortable and secure with the past and while we should look to build on previous experience we do sometimes need encouragement to prise ourselves out of easy ruts and into more uncomfortable challenges. This is a vital part of preparing for the future and for coping with contemporary academic work.

10

A Final Word: A Better Working Life

> This is the true joy in life, the being used for a purpose recognized by yourself as a mighty one; the being a force of nature, instead of a feverish, selfish little clod of ailments and grievances complaining that the world will not devote itself to making you happy.
>
> (George Bernard Shaw, *Man and Superman*)

Working with paradox

In the preceding four chapters, it has been argued that in order to work effectively, a series of tensions need to be balanced: vision and reality; individuality and collaboration; reward and accountability; valuing the past and being open to the future. The situations in which these tensions were explored will have been familiar to most readers: merging departments; new colleagues with different experiences and expectations; demands to do more research as well as to be more efficient; and the constant pressure to demonstrate accountability.

In each of the four case-study chapters, the focus was on one pair of tensions and there is value in modelling, analysing and unpacking the dimensions relevant to each pair of tensions separately; it helps to focus on salient issues and thereby develop useful principles to guide practice. To work with too many pairs of tensions within each case study would likely have been confusing. The truth is, however, that several pairs of tensions do exist within most situations – and it *is* confusing. In book chapters, it is easier to simplify and to focus on issues within fixed perimeters. In real life it is harder.

Dealing with real life and work may be harder but similar principles apply. When things look overwhelming we are told by Senge (1992: 128) that it is necessary to see through the complexity in order to practise the fifth discipline of 'systems thinking' (see p. 67), and thereby bring into focus the big picture, that is, the larger system at work within the organization or department. When the larger system is examined, then it is easier to see what is important, what is not so important and what should not be compromised. Short-term gains can then be seen for what they are.

If we look back to the case studies, we can see that very often staff are working with several tensions all at once. Let us consider just one of the chapters, Chapter 8, for instance. Here, the focus was on balancing accountability and reward. The new head of department worked to find a way to have staff document their achievements in teaching and to embark on more robust research careers whilst he worked to ensure that he guided and acknowledged their achievements. But another tension or paradox was attended to in this chapter. The new head came in with ideas about improving research performance and documenting teaching which were, initially, at odds with the views of many of the staff. A good deal of work by both the new head and his staff went into bringing together the different positions and balancing the leaders' vision with the reality of the staff experience.

In all of the case studies, the staff worked with several sets of tensions or paradoxes. Charles Handy (1996: 47) in his book *The Empty Raincoat: Making Sense of the Future*, tells us that paradoxes do not have to be resolved, only managed. When we think about it, this is exactly so. The tensions in the case studies were not so much resolved as handled. The age-old adage that you can have 'too much of a good thing' is exactly represented in this handling or balancing. As we saw in the previous chapters, collaboration needs robust individualism to work; visions cannot work unless they are informed by the reality of day-to-day experience; reward becomes facile unless charged with accountability and the virtue of the past can only remain enchanting when balanced against the demands of the future. New situations, experiences and times highlight their own paradoxes. The tensions and paradoxes in the new age of higher education confront us now and they have to be managed.

The essential task which we as academic staff face in doing this balancing is a learning task. We need to recognize that the knowledge and insights and experience we have so far acquired, as professional academic staff, valuable as they might be, are probably insufficient in the present changing circumstances. We have to be open to finding new ways of working within the changed environment; new ways of working with our colleagues who are also trying to cope with the changes; and new ways of working with our students, many of whom will be unfamiliar with the university as we have known it.

Learning for academic staff and their universities

Let us remind ourselves what has been said about learning earlier. Two literatures on learning were considered: the first on student learning; the second on learning organizations. A central message of the student learning literature was that students learn in different ways and the best way – the most productive and most satisfying way – occurs when students take responsibility for their learning and when they believe that their learning matters. It matters because they need to grow and develop and master and contribute to the thing they are learning, as well as needing to pass exams and gain certification.

We have also discovered from the student learning literature that the context in which students study and learn is critical. It can be a powerful force for encouraging them to take ownership and control of their learning or it can be the reverse. The student learning literature, however, is aimed at improving teaching and encouraging academic staff to support the learning process. It spells out the most favourable context for this to happen and it is difficult to defend our claim on professionalism if we fail to attend to our responsibility in this respect. In the end, however, students are responsible for their own learning. Countless students learn well in very poor teaching and learning contexts and countless students fail to learn in good ones. The point to be highlighted is that learners – be they students or academic staff – are *not* helpless puppets of the environment. They *can* help themselves and make a difference.

This message of the individual being responsible for their own learning is strongly highlighted in the learning organization literature. This literature and, in particular, the work of Peter Senge examined in Chapter 4, emphasizes that organizations learn through the individual learning of their staff. Very often, however, very little learning goes on because the organization obstructs, rather than supports, learning. The aim of the learning organization literature is to help people within organizations to overcome such systems and to work with, rather than against, each other.

Senge suggests that there are five disciplines, or qualities, essential for the staff of a learning organization to develop. These are:

- *personal mastery*, developing a personal vision and having faith in one's own ability to make a difference within the organization;
- *mental models*, understanding the way oneself and one's colleagues think and reason;
- *shared vision*, aligning one's own aims and ambitions with those of one's colleagues;
- *team learning*, working with colleagues to go beyond one's own way of seeing; and, finally,
- *systems thinking* which involves seeing one's work unit as systems of a larger whole and understanding how what happens in one affects what goes on elsewhere.

Senge emphasizes the first discipline, personal mastery, and the last, systems thinking, as being the most critical. Personal mastery is the starting-point, the point of personal commitment and vision, and the other, systems thinking, provides a way of reading the larger environment and making sense of experiences within the environment as a whole.

Personal mastery and systems thinking will undoubtedly be beneficial for academic staff as they face the changed higher education system and the numerous paradoxes of their new work. Those staff who work towards something they believe in and something they want to contribute to and who have also checked that their goals are not at odds with trends in the larger environment are the ones who will likely reap some success and satisfaction in their new work. The success and satisfaction may be limited or constrained, but it will be palpable. It will mean a working life which has notable elements of satisfaction rather than one which has notable elements of despair. This is important – for we have only one life.

Academic staff sometimes believe that to relinquish things they once valued and to focus on something which is achievable is a sell-out. They staunchly remain committed to ways of working with colleagues and students which in the current climate become increasingly difficult to maintain. Perhaps there is some virtue in this position and if academic staff can find a way of preserving what is valued and proven within current constraints, then they should be encouraged to do so.

It must be remembered, however, that as I write, the newspapers tell me there are grape growers in France and olive growers in Greece and sheep farmers in Australia who are all fighting changes in technologies and trends and markets and are maintaining that the proposed changes will bring devastating and unacceptable consequences on social systems and on the quality of products. They are likely right, a good deal will be lost, and maybe it is important that each generation be made aware of what it is losing, but in the end, industries – be they farming or education – respond to the times and move on. Academic staff have as much a responsibility to ensure that the best ways forward are found, as they do to ensuring that the good things which can be preserved are not lost.

Stories in the universities

As teachers, we know that if we wish to learn from students and, therefore, help them to learn, we must listen to them. As a developer of academic staff, I know, that likewise, we must listen to academic staff to help them to learn and to change. I thus conclude with three salient stories from academic staff themselves. The first comes from the director of personnel of a university which has recently experienced its first round of compulsory redundancies.

The director of personnel

The director of personnel began his story by quoting a German proverb: 'A great war leaves a country with three armies: an army of cripples, an army of mourners and an army of thieves.' He explained that the university had won a considerable battle and he had been a major player in this battle. They had bargained a package for academic staff which included a 10 per cent increase in salaries for the right to enforce redundancies. The consequences of winning this battle were more disruptive and far-reaching than he, or the university, had ever imagined. The university had established schemes and plans to help those staff who were leaving but they had done nothing to assist those staff who remained – and those staff who remained were bitter, shell-shocked, drained of commitment and enthusiasm. Not exactly what was required to drive the new, lean, efficient university.

This director had explored the literature in the area and found that it was common for those remaining to experience guilt that they still had their job; resentment at what had happened to their colleagues; anxiety about what might happen to them; self-absorption around their own future; and stress-related illnesses. He repeated that it seemed as though the university were now run by these three armies of the German proverb: the army of cripples, the mourners and the thieves. After three months, the director himself decided to join the ranks of those leaving and took early retirement (he was 56-years-old). He argued that to help staff pull themselves and the university through this crisis would require more inner resources than he felt capable of being able to give. There may seem little which is positive in this story, but let us not be too hasty to come to this decision. There is more to tell – and this will be done later.

The head of department

The second story, from a colleague and a head of department, is very different, though on the face of it, not obviously more positive. The head had been charged with making significant changes to the degree course. He was to turn the course, a general Social Science course, into a vocational course and he had to attract a different type of student and, therefore, had to provide a different sort of content and teaching. I knew his task and the challenges he faced and believed him to be making good headway. When we met, he began to report progress but soon moved on to an issue which was causing him deep concern. Encouraging academic staff to change had been more than he had bargained for.

Defensiveness, he complained, was the most universal and the most damaging response he had confronted over the year (this issue has been addressed in Chapters 6 and 7). Defensiveness was the characteristic gesture of all of his staff when faced with any criticism or proposal for change no matter how carefully presented and this reaction meant that everything took between two and twenty times as long to move along and when things finally did happen, they would eventually be undermined in some way. Although the staff expected the students to open themselves to scrutiny and although the staff themselves would open their research to the scrutiny of colleagues, when it came to changes in day-to-day work, the staff were fierce in their self-defence. In some cases, the head argued, this defensiveness moved into clinically-definable paranoia. Even the simplest and most innocuous suggestions were seen to come from sinister motives. He gave an example of the Christmas party proposal which had been circulated to all staff and which had excited a flurry of questions such as: Who suggested this? Why is it being held at this time, in this place? Who has been invited? What will be said formally? What does it really signify and what is the ulterior motive?

What do these stories tell us?

Both of these stories tells us something which is believable and which is necessary to consider when reflecting on our work as academic staff, but each does so with a particular slant. The first of the stories presents academic staff as victims – and, indeed, we often feel and see ourselves this way. The second story sees us as villains and, whilst we may never see ourselves that way, we know for sure it is the truth for some – if not a good many – of our colleagues. Stories like this become embellished and become part of the mythology of contemporary academic work when emotions run high and satisfaction is low. We caught a good many glimpses of such stories in the academic staff survey reported in Chapter 2.

Engaging and fashionable as such stories might be, it is important to realize that they are neither particularly helpful for those of us who want to make the most of our working life – nor are they the only stories to tell.

If we take the situation in the first university, where the director of personnel felt he could go on no longer, the university, its departments and remaining staff *did* continue and *did* actually accomplish some significant achievements. At the institutional level, the university's overall scores on the Course Experience Questionnaire (see Chapter 3) were among the highest in the country. This evidence of good teaching and concern for students by staff was further endorsed by a large number of national teaching grants (awarded in Australia by CUTSD, the Committee of University Teaching and Staff Development). At the course level, three new interdisciplinary courses were developed and two received record demands from students at a time when demand, nationally, was down. At the individual level, there were personal promotions and the winning of grants and scholarships just as there had been in other years. It may have been the right decision for the director of personnel to leave, but it does not mean that this was the end of either the work or the progress in this university. In small and sometimes not so small ways, the academic staff rebuilt or continued their working lives and although there was undeniably much grief, there was also much achievement.

In the second story, the frustrations of the head of department were clear – but on closer examination, so were the achievements. The new course was enrolling its first cohort of students. The demand for the course was healthy and, during the development of the course, the academic staff had forged some useful partnerships and strong teaching teams had developed at each year level. When I spoke with another member of staff about progress and outcomes, there was no such bitterness – apprehension perhaps – but also excitement and enthusiasm in goodly quantities.

The lecturer

There is one final story. It tells us how the way in which academic staff are employed is changing. It is told because it is clear that changes in academic employment patterns will have to be confronted, even though the staff in my own survey did not attend to them. Also, it is a particularly courageous story of someone who, until recently, often laughingly described herself as 'one of the also-rans'.

The story involves a long-standing personal friend, Lisa, who was employed at a new university. At the university all permanent staff, both academic and general, were invited to apply for a severance package. If the university got enough takers, then there would be no forced redundancies. It was expected, however, that in some departments the size of budget shortfalls would be such that forced redundancies would be inevitable and the education department was one such department.

Lisa was a senior lecturer in the department for twelve years and was now 46-years-old. She had joined as a lecturer when the then small college had been a college of education. She had loved teaching and teaching young teachers had been an especial joy to her. Steadily, however, the numbers of students had dropped; subjects had been cut and, eventually, the major course in which she taught was discontinued. She, like all of the staff in her department, had to diversify; for example, moving into work-based training; spending time overseas teaching the course to overseas students where there were still healthy enrolments. Lisa had also been told to develop some research expertise, and she felt particularly worried and threatened by this, since she had neither inclination for, nor experience of, research of any sort. Overall, she felt that the things which she was good at were no longer valued. She readily admitted that she only came to work to pay the mortgage. She did what was asked of her but there was little satisfaction and a good deal of frustration and anxiety in her work.

When the severance package was offered she thought about it, but decided against it. She believed that she could not afford to leave. She had a mortgage and she was divorced with two teenage children. It was irresponsible to even consider it. Some weeks later, however, the head of department called Lisa into his office. There had been only two staff (out of ten) willing to take the package. Another two positions had to be lost and Lisa would almost certainly be one of the staff targeted. The financial benefits of taking the package, as opposed to being declared redundant, were considerable. Also, she was told that it was likely that the department would want to re-employ her on a one-year contract if she were willing to take the package.

Some of Lisa's colleagues told her that she was being manipulated and that she should make the university sack her. However, Lisa felt ill-prepared for the inevitable battle. In addition, the subject the head was suggesting that she might be re-engaged to teach on a casual basis looked attractive. The department was being asked to teach an Italian language and culture subject into another department's degree course. Lisa had taught and enjoyed teaching a similar subject some years previously. She was also Italian by birth and had lived in Rome until she was 10 years' old.

Lisa sought professional, personal and financial advice from all quarters. All the advice pointed towards taking the package and thinking positively about finding additional work. At this stage, Lisa set her hopes that the half-promised contract position would materialize. She knew that with this, and money from the package, she would be able to manage for at least another year. When the offer of the contract came a couple of weeks later and when she discovered that it was for three days and not the two days which she had expected, her spirits began to lift.

Straightaway, Lisa asked if she could see the curriculum she was to teach in order to prepare herself – and it became clear that a curriculum did not exist. Within a week, Lisa was asked to undertake an additional contract – that of developing the non-existent curriculum – and she accepted. It was agreed that this additional work would be the equivalent of ten working days. Lisa's car needed repairing, so she negotiated for a single fee for the curriculum development. In less than three weeks, Lisa received her first piece of income, her car was back on the road and her spirits started to rise even further.

Redundancy, particularly for academic staff who have become used to the idea of tenure, is a great shock. It is a great tribute to the resilience and personal determination of Lisa that one year later she is optimistic and confident, in fact, she is urging her former colleagues to take her example and get out of a job they claim to find so unsatisfying and complain about so much. She jokes that if she can do it – and she is only an 'also-ran' – then they certainly can!

Understandably, Lisa's main concern has been paying her way and she still has concerns in this respect, but she now feels much more positive about her ability to win work and to earn money. Probably much more so than she did when she was 'permanently' employed. She has now developed a personal portfolio of three teaching contracts: one with her former university teaching the Italian language and culture subject; one with a local high school teaching Italian to senior girls; and one doing English language training with immigrant employees of a local firm and their families. She enjoys the variety in her work, and despite the fact her future is in many ways more precarious than previously, she now feels more in control of her environment:

> I now have self-confidence and feel as though I have something to offer. Part of the problem was that over the years I'd lost so much confidence. It seemed nothing I could do was of value anymore so I

> couldn't believe that I'd get another job or win any contracts. But that's not been the case.

For academic staff to work as independent consultants to a range of employers may be a novel idea for many of us, but for many more it is not. At the present time, in Australia, around half of academic staff are employed on a casual or contract basis. In the UK, the figure is similar. In some universities, the percentage of permanent staff is as low as 35 per cent and the figure is a decreasing one (Coaldrake 1998). Many part-time and casual staff work for wages with just one institution, but the trend, both among the very experienced who take early retirement and among the very young who by necessity think differently about potential career paths, is to offer services and experience to a number of clients and charge fees rather than be paid wages.

A research assistant I employed on a casual basis recently told me that at this time in his life he did not want a permanent job. He enjoyed the flexibility of working for several months and then doing his own thing – in this case writing a novel. He also believed that when the time did come for him to want to settle down to a more traditional way of life, he would then be able to show that he had a record of repeatedly winning short-term contracts, of being able to manage the demands of several clients and of constantly giving value for money. These aspects would be the best possible reference.

Conclusion

All organizations – not just universities – are restructuring themselves into smaller, tighter, businesses. This means not just changes in the way staff work, but also changes in the way in which the staff are being employed. Increasingly, universities get things done by employing fewer permanent staff and tendering contracts for specific products or services. There is undoubtedly a limit to the extent to which this can be done and, undoubtedly, much is being lost when this happens, but this trend will continue and, as we have seen, will bring opportunities as well as anxiety to our colleagues.

Few of us will be able to embrace such radically different ways of working, at least not in the short term. However, our ways of working are changing and we do have to respond. We could wait for a great leader to step forward and guide us, or a new environment to emerge to support us, but we could wait for a long time. In the end, it comes down to us. It comes down to taking advantage of opportunities to learn and grow which are out there – or focusing on the negatives and the frustrations which are also certainly out there. In the end the choice is ours.

Bibliography

Adair, J. (1996) *Effective Motivation.* London: Pan Books.

Ainley, J. and Long, M. (1995) *The 1994 Course Experience Questionnaire.* Melbourne, Victoria: Graduate Careers Council of Australia.

Altbach, P. (ed.) (1997) *The International Academic Profession: Portraits of 14 Countries.* Carnegie Foundation, San Francisco: Jossey-Bass.

Argyris, C. (1985) *Strategy, Change and Defensive Routines.* London: Pitman.

Argyris, C. and Schön, D.A. (1978) *Organisational Learning: A Theory of Action Perspective.* Wokingham: Addison-Wesley.

Ashenden, D. and Milligan, S. (1995) *Good Universities Guide to Australian Universities and Other Higher Education Institutions.* Melbourne: Mandarin.

Baldwin, G. (1996) First among peers: An essay on academic leadership. *HERDSA News,* 18, 6–9.

Barnet, R. (1997) Still breathing. *Times Higher Education Supplement,* 30 May.

Becher, T. (1989) *Academic Tribes and Territories: Intellectual Enquiry and the Cultures of Disciplines.* Buckingham: Open University Press.

Becker, H.S., Geer, B. and Hughes, E.C. (1968) *Making the Grade: The Academic Side of College Life.* New York: John Wiley.

Benjamin, J. (1997) Academic Staff's Conceptions of and Approaches to Collaboration in the Teaching of Large First-year University Courses. Paper presented at the Annual Conference of the Higher Education Research and Development of Australasia (HERDSA), July, Glenelg, South Australia.

Bennis, W. (1989) *On Becoming a Leader.* London: Business Books.

Biggs, J.B. (1996a) Assessing learning quality: Reconciling institutional, staff and educational demands. *Assessment and Evaluation in Higher Education,* 21, 5–15.

Biggs, J.B. (1996b) Enhancing teaching through constructive alignment. *Higher Education,* 32, 347–64.

Bland, C.J. and Ruffin, M.T. (1992) Characteristics of a productive research environment: Literature review. *Academic Medicine,* 67, 385–97.

Boice, R. (1992) *The New Faculty Member. Supporting and Fostering Professional Development.* San Francisco: Jossey-Bass.

Boyer, E.L. (1990) *Scholarship Reconsidered: Priorities of the Professoriate.* Princeton: Carnegie Foundation for the Advancement of Teaching.

Boyer, E.L., Altbach, P.G. and Whitelaw, M.J. (1994) *The Academic Profession: An International Perspective.* Princeton: Carnegie Foundation for the Advancement of Teaching.

Bridges, W. (1991) *Managing Transitions: Making the Most of Change.* Reading, Massachusetts: Addison-Wesley.

Bright, D. and Williamson, B. (1995) Managing and rewarding performance. In D. Warner and E. Crosthwaite (eds) *Human Resource Management in Higher and Further Education.* Buckingham: SRHE and Open University Press.

Brown, R. (1997) Questions of responsibility. *Times Higher Education Supplement,* 19 December.

Bruner, J.S. (1966) *Toward a Theory of Instruction.* Cambridge, Massachusetts: Harvard University Press.

Candy, P., Crebert, G. and O'Leary, J. (1994) *Developing Lifelong Learners Through Undergraduate Education.* National Board of Employment, Education and Training (NBEET) (Commissioned Report No. 28). Canberra: Australian Government Publishing Service (AGPS).

Clark, B.R. (1995) Complexity and differentiation: The growing problem of university integration. In D.D. Dill and B. Sporn (eds) *Emerging Patterns of Social Demand and University Reform: Through a Glass Darkly.* Paris: IAU Press/Pergamon.

Coaldrake, P. (1998) Comments on Roderick West's discussion paper, 'Learning for Life'. *Higher Education Research and Development,* 17.

Dahlgren, L.O. (1984) Outcomes of learning. In F. Marton, D. Hounsell and N.J. Entwistle (eds) *The Experience of Learning Implications for Teaching and Studying in Higher Education,* pp. 19–35. Edinburgh: Scottish Academic Press.

DEET (Department of Employment, Education and Training) (1993) *Business/Higher Education Round Table Report, 1991.* Higher Education Division (National Report on Australia). Canberra: Australian Government Publishing Service (AGPS).

Deming, W.E. (1988) *Out of Crisis.* Massachusetts: MIT, Center for Advanced Engineering Study and Cambridge University Press.

Drucker, P.F. (1990) *The New Realities.* London: Heinemann Professional Publishing.

Eble, K.E. (1988) *The Craft of Teaching,* 2nd edn. San Francisco: Jossey-Bass.

Edgerton, R., Hutchings, P. and Quinlan, K. (1991) *The Teaching Portfolio: Capturing the Scholarship in Teaching.* Washington, DC: American Association for Higher Education.

Egan, G. (1995) A clear path to peak performance. *People Management,* 18 May, 34–7.

Entwistle, N. and Ramsden, P. (1983) *Understanding Student Learning.* London: Croom Helm.

Entwistle, N. and Wilson, J.D. (1977) *Degrees of Excellence 'The Academic Acehivement Game'.* London: Hodder and Stoughton.

Fisher, S. (1995) *Stress in Academic Life: The Mental Assembly Line.* Buckingham: SRHE and Open University Press.

Fritz, R. (1989) *The Path of Least Resistance.* New York: Fawcett-Columbine.

Fullan, M. (1994) *Change Forces: Probing the Depths of Educational Reform.* London: Falmer Press.

Gibbs, G. (1992) *Assessing More Students.* London: Polytechnics and Colleges Funding Council.

Habeshaw, S., Habeshaw, T. and Gibbs, G. (1984) *53 Interesting Things to Do in Your Seminars and Tutorials.* Bristol: Technical and Educational Services Limited.

Halsey, A.H. (1992) *Decline of Donnish Dominion.* Oxford: Clarendon Press.

Handy, C. (1996) *The Empty Raincoat: Making Sense of the Future.* London: Random House.

Harvey, L. (1995) Beyond TQM. *Quality in Higher Education,* 1, 123–46.

Hickman, Craig (1992) *Mind of a Manager, Soul of a Leader.* New York: John Wiley and Sons.

Hodgson, V. (1984) Learning from lectures. In F. Marton, D. Hounsell and N.J. Entwistle (eds) *The Experience of Learning Implications for Teaching and Studying in Higher Education.* Edinburgh: Scottish Academic Press.

Ince, M. (1997) Survey reveals crisis fears. *Times Higher Education Supplement,* 10 January.

Kouzes, J.M. and Posner, B.Z. (1995) *The Leadership Challenge.* San Francisco: Jossey-Bass.

Laurillard, D. (1984) Learning from problem-solving. In F. Marton, D. Hounsell and N.J. Entwistle (eds) *The Experience of Learning Implications for Teaching and Studying in Higher Education,* pp. 126–44. Edinburgh: Scottish Academic Press.

Lessing, D. (1986) *Prisons We Chose to Live Inside.* Toronto: CBC Enterprises.

Lowe, I. (1994) *Our Universities are Turning Us Into the 'Ignorant Country'.* Sydney: University of New South Wales Press.

Marginson, S. (1993) *Education and Public Policy in Australia.* Melbourne: Cambridge University Press.

Marginson, S. (1997) How free is academic freedom? *Higher Education Research and Development,* 16, 359–69.

Martin, E. and Balla, M. (1991) Conceptions of teaching and implications for learning. *Research and Development in Higher Education,* 13, 298–304.

Martin, E. and Ramsden, P. (1994) *Effectiveness and Efficiency of Courses in Teaching Methods for Recently Appointed Academic Staff.* Canberra: Australian Government Publishing Service (AGPS).

Martin, E., Prosser, M., Benjamin, J., Trigwell, K. and Ramsden, P. (1997) Heads of academic departments' conceptions of leadership of teaching. In G. Gibbs (ed.) *Improving Student Learning Through Course Design.* Oxford: Oxford Centre for Staff Development.

Marton, F. and Säljö, R. (1976) On qualitative differences in learning. I. Outcome and process. *British Journal of Educational Psychology,* 46, 4–11.

Marton, F. and Booth, S. (1997) *Learning and Awareness.* New Jersey: Lawrence Erlbaum Associates.

Marton, F., Dall'Alba, G. and Beaty, E. (1993) Conceptions of learning. *International Journal of Educational Research,* 19, 277–300.

Marton, F. and Säljö, R. (1997) Approaches to learning. In F. Marton, D. Hounsell and N.J. Entwistle (eds) *The Experience of Learning Implications for Teaching and Studying in Higher Education,* 2nd edn, pp. 39–58. Edinburgh: Scottish Academic Press.

Marton, F., Hounsell, D. and Entwistle, N.J. (eds) (1997) *The Experience of Learning: Implications for Teaching and Studying in Higher Education,* 2nd edn. Edinburgh: Scottish Academic Press.

McInnis, C. (1996) Change and diversity in the work patterns of Australian academics. *Higher Education Management,* 8, 105–17.

McNay, I. (1995) From the collegial academy to the corporate enterprise: The changing cultures of universities. In T. Schuller (ed.) *The Changing University?* Buckingham: SRHE and Open University Press.

Moses, I. (1995) Tensions and tendencies in the management of quality and autonomy in Australian higher education. *Australian Universities Review,* 1, 11–15.

Pascale, R.T. (1990) *Managing on the Edge.* New York: Simon and Schuster; London: Viking.

Patrick, K. (1996) *Internationalising the University, Implications for Teaching and Learning at RMIT* (Report on the Commonwealth Staff Development Fund Internationalisation Project). Melbourne: RMIT University, Educational Program Improvement Group.

Peters, T. (1988) *Thriving on Chaos.* New York: Alfred A. Knopf; London: Macmillan.

Peters, T. and Waterman, R. (1982) *In Search of Excellence.* New York and London: Macmillan.

Prosser, M. and Trigwell, K. (1997) Perceptions of the teaching environment and its relationship to approaches to teaching. *British Journal of Educational Psychology,* 67, 25–35.

Prosser, M., Trigwell, K. and Taylor, P. (1994) A phenomenographic study of academics' conceptions of science learning and teaching. *Learning and Instruction,* 4, 217–31.

Raelin, J.A. (1991) *The Clash of Cultures: Managers Managing Professionals.* Boston: Harvard Business School Press.

Ramsden, P. (1979) Student learning and perceptions of the academic environment. *Higher Education,* 8, 411–28.

Ramsden, P. (1992) *Learning to Teach in Higher Education.* London: Routledge.

Ramsden, P. (1998) *Learning to Lead.* London: Routledge.

Ramsden, P. (1998) What Makes a University Effective? Inaugural Professorial Lecture, April, Institute for Higher Education, Griffith University, Australia.

Ramsden, P. and Entwistle, N.J. (1981) Effects of academic departments on students' approaches to studying. *British Journal of Educational Psychology,* 51, 368–83.

Ramsden, P. and Martin, E. (1996) Recognition of good university teaching: Policies from an Australian study. *Studies in Higher Education,* 21, 299–315.

Ramsden, P., Margetson, D., Martin, E. and Clarke, S. (1995) *Recognising and Rewarding Good Teaching in Australian Higher Education.* Canberra: Australian Government Publishing Service (AGPS).

Ramsden, P., Prosser, M., Trigwell, K. and Martin, E. (1997) Perceptions of Academic Leadership and the Effectiveness of University Teaching. Paper presented at the Annual Conference of the Australian Association for Research in Education, November, Brisbane, Australia.

Reeders, E., Engelhard, M., Horvat, L. and Hough, G. (1996) An Embarrassment of Meanings: A Case Study of the Introduction of a Quality Assurance Scheme. Paper presented at the Annual Conference of the Higher Education Research and Development Society of Australasia (HERDSA), July, Brisbane, Australia.

Roche, V. (1996) The Academic's Progress: Changes and Stages in the Journey. Paper presented at the Annual Conference of the Higher Education Research and Development Society of Australasia (HERDSA), July, Brisbane, Australia.

Rowntree, D. (1977) *Assessing Students.* London: Kogan Page.

Säljö, R. (1979) *Learning in the Learner's Perspective. 1. Some Common-sense Conceptions* (Report No. 76). Gothenberg: Department of Education, University of Gothenburg.

Säljö, R. (1997) Reading and everyday conceptions of knowledge. In F. Marton, D. Hounsell and N.J. Entwistle (eds) *The Experience of Learning Implications for Teaching and Studying in Higher Education,* 2nd edn, pp. 89–105. Edinburgh: Scottish Academic Press.

Samuelowicz, K. and Bain, J.D. (1992) Conceptions of teaching held by teachers. *Higher Education,* 24, 93–112.

Sarros, J.C., Gmelch, W.H. and Tanewski, G.A. (1996) *Higher Education Research and Development,* 16, 65–88.

Sawyer, W.W. (1943) *Mathematician's Delight.* Harmondsworth: Penguin.

Schön, D. (1983) *The Reflective Practioner: How Professionals Think in Action.* New York: Basic Books.

Schrage, M. (1995) *No More Teams! Mastering the Dynamics of Creative Collaboration.* New York: Currency Doubleday.

Scott, P. (1995) *The Meanings of Mass Higher Education.* Buckingham: SRHE and Open University Press.

Senge, P. (1992) *The Fifth Discipline: The Art and Practice of the Learning Organisation.* New York: Doubleday.

Sheehan, B.A. and Welch, A.R. (1996) *The Academic Profession in Australia.* Canberra: Australian Government Publishing Service (AGPS).

Temponi, I. and Martin E. (1997) Theory and practice in management accounting for students. Paper presented at the Higher Education, Research and Development Society of Australasia conference, Adelaide, South Australia.

The Australian, May 6, 1996, 'Working for Australia'.

Trigwell, K. and Prosser, M. (1996a) Congruence between intention and strategy in science teachers' approach to teaching. *Higher Education,* 32, 77–87.

Trigwell, K. and Prosser, M. (1996b) Changing approaches to teaching: A relational perspective. *Studies in Higher Education,* 21, 275–84.

Trigwell, K., Prosser, M. and Waterhouse, F. Relations between teachers' approaches to teaching and student approaches to learning. *Higher Education* (in press).

Waterman, R. (1987) *The Renewal Factor.* New York: Bantam.

Weber, M. (1947) *The Sociology of Charismatic Authority.* New York: Oxford University Press.

Whitehead, A.N. (1967) *The Aims of Education and Other Essays.* London: Ernest Benn (first published by Williams and Northgate in 1932).

Wilson, K., Lizzio, A. and Ramsden, P. (1997) The development, validation and application of the Course Experience Questionnaire. *Studies in Higher Education,* 22, 3–25.

Index

The Society for Research into Higher Education

The Society for Research into Higher Education exists to stimulate and coordinate research into all aspects of higher education. It aims to improve the quality of higher education through the encouragement of debate and publication on issues of policy, on the organization and management of higher education institutions, and on the curriculum and teaching methods.

The Society's income is derived from subscriptions, sales of its books and journals, conference fees and grants. It receives no subsidies, and is wholly independent. Its individual members include teachers, researchers, managers and students. Its corporate members are institutions of higher education, research institutes, professional, industrial and governmental bodies. Members are not only from the UK, but from elsewhere in Europe, from America, Canada and Australasia, and it regards its international work as among its most important activities.

Under the imprint *SRHE & Open University Press*, the Society is a specialist publisher of research, having over 70 titles in print. The Editorial Board of the Society's Imprint seeks authoritative research or study in the above fields. It offers competitive royalties, a highly recognizable format in both hardback and paperback and the worldwide reputation of the Open University Press.

The Society also publishes *Studies in Higher Education* (three times a year), which is mainly concerned with academic issues, *Higher Education Quarterly* (formerly *Universities Quarterly*), mainly concerned with policy issues, *Research into Higher Education Abstracts* (three times a year), and *SRHE News* (four times a year).

The society holds a major annual conference in December, jointly with an institution of higher education. In 1996 the topic was 'Working in Higher Education' at University of Wales, Cardiff. In 1997 it was 'Beyond the First Degree' at the University of Warwick and in 1998 it was 'The Globalization of Higher Education' at the University of Lancaster. The 1999 conference will be on the topic of higher education and its communities at UMIST.

The Society's committees, study groups and networks are run by the members. The networks at present include:

Access
Curriculum Development
Disability
Eastern European
Funding
Legal Education
Mentoring
Postgraduate Issues
Quality
Quantitative Studies
Student Development
Vocational Qualifications

Benefits to members

Individual

Individual members receive:

- *SRHE News*, the Society's publications list, conference details and other material included in mailings.
- Greatly reduced rates for *Studies in Higher Education* and *Higher Education Quarterly*.
- A 35 per cent discount on all SRHE & Open University Press publications.
- Free copies of the Procedings – commissioned papers on the theme of the Annual Conference.
- Free copies of *Research into Higher Education Abstracts*.
- Reduced rates for the annual conference.
- Extensive contacts and scope for facilitating initiatives.
- Free copies of the *Register of Members' Research Interests*.
- Membership of the Society's networks.

Corporate

Corporate members receive:

- Benefits of individual members, plus:
- Free copies of *Studies in Higher Education*.
- Unlimited copies of the Society's publications at reduced rates.
- Reduced rates for the annual conference.
- The right to submit applications for the Society's research grants.
- The right to use the Society's facility for supplying statistical HESA data for purposes of research.

SRHE

Membership details: SRHE, 3 Devonshire Street, London W1N 2BA, UK. Tel: 0171 637 2766. Fax: 0171 637 2781.
email: srhe@mailbox.ulcc.ac.uk
World Wide Web: http://www.srhe.ac.uk./srhe/
Catalogue: SRHE & Open University Press, Celtic Court, 22 Ballmoor, Buckingham MK18 1XW. Tel: 01280 823388.
Fax: 01280 823233. email: enquiries@openup.co.uk

ACADEMICS RESPONDING TO CHANGE
NEW HIGHER EDUCATION FRAMEWORKS AND ACADEMIC CULTURES

Paul R. Trowler

Paul R. Trowler takes a close took inside one British university to explore how academic staff at the ground level respond to changes in higher education. During the period of this study there was a remarkably rapid expansion in student numbers and, at the same time, a shrinking unit of resource. Meanwhile new systems and structures were being put in place, particularly those associated with the 'credit framework': the constellation of features associated with the assignment of credit value to assessed learning, including modularity, franchising and the accreditation of prior learning. The book explores the nature and effects of academics' responses to these changes and develops a framework for explaining these responses. It offers a valuable insight into change in higher education and highlights some of the processes which lead to policy outcomes being rather different from the intentions of policy-makers.

Contents

208pp 0 335 19934 8 (Paperback) 0 335 19935 6 (Hardback)

MANAGING ACADEMIC STAFF IN CHANGING UNIVERSITY SYSTEMS

David Farnham (ed.)

This book provides a contemporary and international analysis of how academic staff in universities are currently managed. It reviews recent developments in higher education policy in fifteen selected countries and examines their impacts on the academic profession. Whilst rates of change differ, the massifying, marketizing and managerializing of higher education are universal, international phenomena. With strategic attempts being made to re-engineer an increasingly diverse, functionally-differentiated academic profession, there are signs of an emerging but uneven 'flexi-university' model of academic employment. Indicators of this phenomenon include the casualizing of academic work, widening pay differentials, institutional pay scales, decentralized pay bargaining and, in some cases, the individualizing of the employment relationship.

This is a comprehensive reference work and a key resource for university managers and for all those interested in higher education policy and practice.

Contents

384pp 0 335 19961 5 (Hardback)

THE ADULT UNIVERSITY

Etienne Bourgeois, Chris Duke, Jean-Luc Guyot and Barbara Merrill

In most universities there are now more adults as students than young people straight from school. Yet many universities continue to act as if no such change had taken place. *The Adult University* examines theoretically and practically key issues of broader participation in highter education. It asks:

- What are university access policies and how do they connect with practice; do universities behave in ways which encourage or thwart wider access?
- How do adults experience universities; and how far do universities adapt to assist adults?
- What can universities realistically do to improve both the access to and experience of university for adults.

This is a genuinely international study by a transnational team which is grounded in research into two institutions in two major European university traditions. Its focus is both on national systems and local interactions, on macro level policy and students' own voices.

The Adult University is essential reading for all those interested in the development of our mass higher education system. It points to ways in which individual universities and the system of higher education could and should evolve in advanced industrial societies.

Contents

c.208pp 0 335 19907 0 (Paperback) 0 335 19908 9 (Hardback)